ALLIANCE AND CONDEMNATION

———

ALIANZA Y CONDENA

Alliance and Condemnation

———

Alianza y condena

Claudio Rodríguez

Translated and with an Introduction by
PHILIP W. SILVER

Claudio Rodríguez (1934-1999) is the outstanding Spanish poet of the late twentieth century. At nineteen he won the *Premio Adonais de Poesía* for his first book, *Don de la ebriedad* (1953). For *Alianza y condena* he received the prestigious *Premio de la Crítica* (1966), and for subsequent works he received the *Premio Nacional de Poesía* (1983) and the *Premio de las Letras de Castilla y León* (1986). In 1987 he was elected to the Real Academia Española. In 1993 he was awarded both the *Premio Príncipe de Asturias* and the *Premio Reina Sofía de Poesía Iberoamericana.*

Philip W. Silver is a professor emeritus, Columbia University, and the author of several books, including *Ruin and Restitution: Reinterpreting Romanticism in Spain.*

Swan Isle Press, Chicago 60640-8790

Printed in the United States of America
First Edition

14 15 16 17 18   1 2 3 4 5
ISBN-13: 978-0-9833220-2-3 (paperback)

Alianza y condena (1965) was originally published by Revista de Occidente, Madrid.

Translations are based on *Claudio Rodríguez, Poesía completa* (1953–1991) (Barcelona: Tusquets, colección *Marginales* 198 *Nuevos Textos Sagrados,* 2001).

Swan Isle Press wishes to acknowledge the generous collaboration of Clara Miranda for her support in preparing this edition; Concha González de Garayo at Biblioteca Pública Municipal de Zamora (Claudio Rodríguez Archives); and Iñaki Serraller Vizcaino for his photograph of Philip Silver.

Library of Congress Cataloging-in-Publication Data

Rodríguez, Claudio,
  [Alianza y condena. English & Spanish]
  Alliance and Condemnation / Alianza y Condena / Claudio Rodríguez; translated and with an introduction by Philip W. Silver.
     p. cm.
  Includes bibliographical references.
ISBN 978-0-9833220-2-3 (paperback)
1. Silver, Philip W., 1932- translator.   II. Title.
PQ6633.O34A713 2014
  861'.64—DC23

                        2014005253

Swan Isle Press gratefully acknowledges that this edition was made possible in part with the generous support of:

    MICHELLE MERCER AND BRUCE GOLDEN
    FRANCIS J. HIGGINS
    DEBRA S. RADE
    EUROPE BAY GIVING TRUST

www.swanislepress.com

For Clara
Para Clara

CONTENTS

Claudio Rodríguez (1934-1999) was born in the provincial capital of Zamora, but lived most of his life in Madrid. He received the degree of Licenciado in Romance Philology from the University of Madrid in 1957. Already a prize-winning poet at age nineteen, he wrote his thesis on the magical aspects of Castilian children's choral songs. In Madrid he also met the Nobel Prize winner, Vicente Aleixandre, who became a lifelong friend and mentor. Then from 1958 until 1964 he taught in England as Spanish lecturer at the universities of Nottingham and Cambridge. In all, between 1953 and 1991, he published five books of poetry. In 1987 he was elected to the Royal Spanish Academy where he served until his death.

As a child, Claudio Rodríguez lived through Spain's Civil War (1936-1939) and the repressive Franco years. But all he re-membered of the war was watching a firing squad with his father. Later, he weathered Spain's bumpy, but in the end spectacular, transition to democracy. As a student he had belonged to the

Spanish Communist Party, but only, as he liked to say, "for about twenty minutes." All this is reflected, obliquely, in his poetry. It may be that his literary success at nineteen brought its own kind of solitude. But there was also, in his youth, a "mystical" experience that provided the impulse for his first book and marked him for the rest of his life; a kind of illumination that recalled those of the nineteenth-century English nature poets such as Wordsworth. What he experienced, he tells us, was a sense of oneness with the night sky, extreme fear and an intense feeling of levitation[1]. Except for the Mystics—St. John of the Cross, St. Theresa—there were no Spanish antecedents for this facet of Claudio Rodríguez's poetry[2].

He was by nature somewhat traditional, liked soccer, bullfights, read three or four newspapers a day, including the conservative ABC, and was not particularly interested in politics. His gestures seemed abrupt, as is often the case with the large and robust, but he was friendly, unsophisticated, a little shy, and loved to amuse his nephews and other children. He also enjoyed giving readings of his poetry, always from the same dog-eared anthology. He was an excellent reader—his voice was strong, emotional, and with a marked lyrical *glissando*. Although graced with a supreme gift of language, he sometimes surprised close friends by asking about the propriety of certain words—for example, whether he should say, in "Witches at Noon," that the witches "piss" or "pee,"

1. See Mercedes Monmany, "Claudio Rodríguez: 'La vida parece y no parece verdadera, es casi como una leyenda,'" *El Europeo*, # 32, May 1991, 76.

2. Despite being a life-long reader of the Mystics' prose and poetry, Rodríguez was always adamant that he was not, in fact or intention, a religious poet.

or whether he could properly use the word *corva* (the back of the knee) instead of the less erotic *pantorrilla* (calf). And he always had time to enjoy his friends, even in his last year when he was dying of cancer and working steadily on *Aventura,* a sixth book he never finished.

In the long periods between one book and the next, there was no sign that he even was a poet— except for a small notebook and the stub of a pencil that he always carried. He never seemed to mind these long fallow periods. He even said that no one was a poet for life, and that older poets should have expiration dates like yogurt. Beginning with *Don de la ebriedad (Gift of Ecstasy)* and for forty years, to the avid poetry reader, to poet friends, students, the common reader, and the media, he was that remarkable human being, a great poet, someone whom the gods had touched. He was unimpeachably forthright in a world not without its literary scalawags, and because he avoided the in-fighting expected of a literary figure, his exalted status —which seemed to surprise and amuse him—became legendary.

As a careful reading of *Alliance and Condemnation* will show, the marrow of Claudio Rodríquez's poetry is far from traditional. It is best understood as converging with one of the two dominant traditions of twentieth century philosophy: existential phenomenology (a philosophy of "life" in which the union of "I" and "my circumstances" is all there is). In this light it is easier to understand how these poems reveal a new poetic realm: that of the poet's "life." Or, as the French philosopher, Gabriel Marcel, would say, his "unmediated immediacy." Is there any specific evidence that Claudio Rodríguez was aware of the radical novelty of his artistic practice?

In his address to the Royal Academy on Miguel Hernández's poetry, he spoke of what he called "poetic participation." This, he explained, takes place in the "spontaneity of life," and "is prior to any apparent divisions." As he said in the Academy address, the poet "must inhabit the pulse and change of life at every moment...." Or, live the temporalization of Being as it flows through and around him. In *Alliance and Condemnation* Claudio Rodríguez writes:

> *I love this light*
> *for its purple, copper hue.*
> *Light that takes shape in me,*
> *that is time in me,*
> *this light that is my life*
> *because it gives me life:*
> *all I ask for my love and my ease.*
>
> ("THIS LIGHT")

In 1997 Claudio Rodríguez and I began to translate his work with a Selected Poems in mind. After his death I put that project aside and, much later, decided instead to translate what I think is his best book, *Alianza y condena*. The present translations were done with a bilingual edition in mind, and are as faithful to the originals as I could make them. However, to this end I often had to lengthen the English translation in an attempt to approximate the cadence, meaning and suggestion of the original poem. I have followed the Spanish syntax closely. Where noun and verb are separated by several intervening clauses, I have followed suit rather than rearrange the word order, since order and disorder are part of Claudio Rodríguez's poetic style. As to the lexicon, only

in a few cases was there a problem. I have left untranslated *Mus,
Tute,* and *cazalla.* The first two are very popular Spanish card
games, as their context makes clear. *Cazalla* is more commonly
called *aguardiente,* and in English, aquavit. As the poem suggests
it is drunk with the morning coffee, or by itself.

Finally, I could not have completed these translations without
the generous help of my wife Cristina Vizcaino Auger, Chris-
topher Maurer, Jan Church, Mikel Azurmendi, Paula Serraller,
and Joan de la Cova. Of course, any mistranslations are my own
doing. Claudio Rodríguez is not always easy to read correctly.
This is why the help of a friend and specialist like Ángel L. Prieto
de Paula has been invaluable.

Philip W. Silver
Maine, 2014

ALLIANCE AND CONDEMNATION

———

ALIANZA Y CONDENA

BRUJAS A MEDIODÍA

(Hacia el conocimiento)

NO son cosas de viejas
ni de agujas sin ojo o alfileres
sin cabeza. No salta,
como sal en la lumbre, este sencillo
sortilegio, este viejo
maleficio. Ni hisopo
para rociar ni vela
de cera virgen necesita. Cada
forma de vida tiene
un punto de cocción, un meteoro
de burbujas. Allí, donde el sorteo
de los sentidos busca
propiedad, allí, donde
se cuaja el ser, en ese
vivo estambre, se aloja
la hechicería. No es tan sólo el cuerpo,
con su leyenda de torpeza, lo que
nos engaña: en la misma
constitución de la materia, en tanta
claridad que es estafa,
guiños, mejunjes, trémulo
carmín, nos trastornan. Y huele
a toca negra y aceitosa, a pura
bruja este mediodía de septiembre
y en los pliegues del aire,

WITCHES AT NOON

(Toward Wisdom)

T H E S E aren't old wives' tales,
eyeless needles
or headless pins. This simple charm,
this old spell doesn't spark
like salt in the fire.
It doesn't need sprinkling with hyssop,
or virgin candle wax. Every form of life
has a boiling point, leaves a meteor
of bubbles. Where the lottery
of the senses searches for something
to possess, where
being takes form, in that
living fabric there is witchcraft.
It isn't only the body
with its legend of clumsiness
that deceives us, in the very constitution
of matter, in so much clarity it's deception,
the winks, potions, trembling
crimson all confound us.
And this September noon
smells of pure witchery,
of black oily wimples;
and in the pleats of the air,
on the altars of space,
there are buried vices, places

en los altares del espacio hay vicios
enterrados, lugares
donde se compra juventud, siniestras
recetas para amores. Y en la tensa
maduración del día, no unos labios
sino secas encías,
nos chupan de la sangre
el rezo y la blasfemia,
el recuerdo, el olvido,
todo aquello que fue sosiego o fiebre.
Como quien lee en un renglón tachado
el arrepentimiento de una vida,
con tesón, con piedad, con fe, aun con odio,
ahora, a mediodía, cuando hace
calor y está apagado
el sabor, contemplamos
el hondo estrago y el tenaz progreso
de las cosas, su eterno
delirio, mientras chillan
las golondrinas de la huida.

La flor del monte, la manteca añeja,
el ombligo de niño, la verbena
de la mañana de San Juan, el manco
muñeco, la resina,
buena para caderas de mujer,
el azafrán, el cardo bajo, la olla
de Talavera con pimienta y vino,
todo lo que es cosa de brujas, cosa
natural, hoy no es nada

where youth is for sale,
and sinister recipes for love.
And in the day's taut ripening
not lips but parched gums
suck prayers and blasphemy
from our blood,
suck memories, forgotten things,
all that was fever or comfort before.
Like someone reading in crossed-out sentences
the repentance of a whole life,
insistently, with pity, faith, even with hate,
now at noon when it's hot
and our taste is dull, we study
the deep ruin, the tenacious progress
of things, their eternal delirium
as swallows shriek
in their receding flight.

Mountain flowers, rancid lard,
an infant's belly-button,
the festival on Saint John's morning,
a doll with a missing arm,
resin to rub on women's hips,
saffron, low thistle, a Talavera
crock with pepper and wine;
today every witch-like thing,
every natural thing,

junto a este aquelarre
de imágenes que, ahora,
cuando los seres dejan poca sombra,
da un reflejo: la vida.
La vida no es reflejo
pero, ¿cuál es su imagen?
Un cuerpo encima de otro
¿siente resurrección o muerte? ¿Cómo
envenenar, lavar
este aire que no es nuestro pulmón?
¿Por qué quien ama nunca
busca verdad, sino que busca dicha?
¿Cómo sin la verdad
puede existir la dicha? He aquí todo.

Pero nosotros nunca
tocamos la sutura,
esa costura (a veces un remiendo,
a veces un bordado),
entre nuestros sentidos y las cosas,
esa fina arenilla
que ya no huele dulce sino a sal,
donde el río y el mar se desembocan,
un eco en otro eco, los escombros
de un sueño en la cal viva
del sueño aquel por el que yo di un mundo
y lo seguiré dando. Entre las ruinas
del sol tiembla
un nido con calor nocturno. Entre
la ignominia de nuestras leyes se alza

is nothing compared to this Witches'
Sabbath of images that now,
when beings cast only
the slenderest shadows,
reflects only this: life.
Life isn't a reflection
but what is its image?
Does one body on top of another
feel resurrection or death?
How can we poison, wash clean,
this air that isn't our lungs?
Why does no lover want truth,
only happiness? How without truth
can there be happiness? That's the point.

But we never
touch the suture,
the seam (sometimes a patch,
sometimes embroidery)
between our senses and things,
the powdery sand,
no longer sweet-smelling but salty,
where rivers and the sea join,
one echo inside another, the rubble
of one dream in the quicklime
of the dream for which I gave a world
and will go on giving. Among the ruins
of the sun a nest warmed by the night
trembles. From the ignominy of our laws
comes a retablo of antique gold and the doctrine

el retablo con viejo
oro y vieja doctrina
de la nueva justicia. ¿En qué mercados
de altas sisas el agua
es vino, el vino sangre, sed la sangre?
¿Por qué aduanas pasa
de contrabando harina
como carne, la carne
como polvo y el polvo
como carne futura?

Esto es cosa de bobos. Un delito
común éste de andar entre pellizcos
de brujas. Porque ellas
no estudian sino bailan
y mean, son amigas
de bodegas. Y ahora,
a mediodía,
si ellas nos besan desde tantas cosas,
¿dónde estará su noche,
dónde sus labios, dónde nuestra boca
para aceptar tanta mentira y tanto
amor?

of a new justice. In what devious markets
is water wine, wine blood
and blood thirst?
What customs house
lets this contraband through:
flour as flesh, flesh
as dust and dust
as future flesh?

A riddle for dunces. A petty
crime, this walking between witches'
pinches, because they don't study
but dance and piss and enjoy
wine cellars. And now at noon
if they kiss us from so many things,
where will their night be, where will
their lips be, where will our mouths be,
to accept so many lies and
so much love?

GESTOS

U N A mirada, un gesto,
cambiarán nuestra vida. Cuando actúa mi mano,
tan sin entendimiento y sin gobierno
pero con errabunda resonancia,
y sondea buscando
calor y compañía en este espacio
en donde tantas otras
han vibrado, ¿qué quiere
decir? Cuántos y cuántos gestos como
un sueño mañanero
pasaron. Como esa
casera mueca de las figurillas
de la baraja, aunque
dejando herida o beso, sólo azar entrañable.
Más luminoso aún que la palabra
nuestro ademán como ella
roído por el tiempo, viejo como la orilla
del río, ¿qué
significa?
¿Por qué desplaza el mismo aire el gesto
de la entrega o del robo,
el que cierra una puerta o el que la abre,
el que da luz o apaga?
¿Por qué es el mismo el giro del brazo cuando siembra
que cuando siega,
el del amor que el del asesinato?

GESTURES

A gaze, a gesture
will change our lives. When my hand moves
with little understanding or control
but with aimless resonance,
and dips down, searching
for warmth and company,
in this space where so many other
hands have wavered, what does it mean?
So many gestures have passed by
like early morning dreams.
Like those homely
grimaces on face cards,
although they leave wounds or a kiss,
they are only affectionate chance.
Even more radiant than words,
although like words eroded by time
and old as a riverbank,
what do they mean?
Why do the gestures of giving
and stealing displace equal volumes of air,
or closing a door as opening it
or turning a light on as off?
Why is the sweep of an arm the same
when sowing as when wielding a scythe,
or the gestures of love the same
as the assassin's?

Nosotros tan gesteros pero tan poco alegres,
raza que sólo supo
tejer banderas, raza de desfiles,
de fantasías y de dinastías,
hagamos otras señas.
No he de leer en cada palma, en cada
movimiento, como antes. No puedo ahora frenar
la rotación inmensa del abrazo
para medir su órbita
y recorrer su emocionada curva.
No, no son tiempos
de mirar con nostalgia
esa estela infinita del paso de los hombres.
Hay mucho que olvidar
y más aún que esperar. Tan silencioso
como el vuelo del búho, un gesto claro,
de sencillo bautizo,
dirá, en un aire nuevo,
su nueva significación, su nuevo
uso. Yo sólo, si es posible,
pido cuando me llegue la hora mala,
la hora de echar de menos tantos gestos queridos,
tener fuerza, encontrarlos
como quien halla un fósil
(acaso una quijada aún con el beso trémulo)
de una raza extinguida.

All of us, so versed in the movement
of hands but so joyless,
a race that only knew how
to weave flags, fond of marching,
of fantasies and dynasties,
let us invent other signs.
I won't read in every palm, every
movement, as before. I can't stop
the immense rotation of an embrace
so as to measure its orbit
and trace its heartfelt curve.
No, these are not times
to look with nostalgia at the infinite wake
of man's passing.
There is so much to forget
and even more to hope for. As silent
as an owl in flight,
a frank gesture simply performed
will announce in a new space
its new meaning and its new manner.
If it's possible, when a sad hour comes,
with nostalgia for so many beloved gestures,
I only ask for the strength to view them
as someone who has found the fossil
(perhaps a jawbone still with a trembling kiss)
of an extinct race.

PORQUE NO POSEEMOS

(La mirada)

I

PORQUE no poseemos,
vemos. La combustión del ojo en esta
hora del día cuando la luz, cruel
de tan veraz, daña
la mirada ya no me trae aquella
sencillez. Ya no sé qué es lo que muere,
qué lo que resucita. Pero miro,
cojo fervor, y la mirada se hace
beso, ya no sé si de amor o traicionero.
Quiere acuñar las cosas,
detener su hosca prisa
de adiós, vestir, cubrir
su feroz desnudez de despedida
con lo que sea: con esa membrana
delicada del aire,
aunque fuera tan sólo
con la sutil ternura
del velo que separa las celdillas
de la granada. Quiere untar su aceite,
denso de juventud y de fatiga,
en tantos goznes luminosos que abre
la realidad, entrar
dejando allí, en alcobas tan fecundas,

BECAUSE WE DON'T POSSESS

(The Gaze)

I

BECAUSE we don't possess,
we see. The glint of the eyes
at this hour of day, when the light
with cruel veracity hurts our gaze,
no longer brings me that former
simplicity. I can no longer tell
what's dying, what's being revived.
But I stare with increasing fervor
and my gaze becomes a kiss,
I don't know if of love or betrayal.
It wants to put its mark on things,
halt their brusque goodbye,
dress, cover the fierce nakedness
of their leaving with anything at all:
with that delicate membrane of air,
even with only the subtle tenderness
of film between pomegranate cells.
It wants to spread its oil, heavy
with youth and fatigue, on all the luminous
hinges that reality opens; to enter
and place there, in those fertile chambers,
its lees and its leavings,
its nest and its storm,

su poso y su despojo,
su nido y su tormenta,
sin poder habitarlas. Qué mirada
oscura viendo cosas
tan claras. Mira, mira:
allí sube humo, empiezan
a salir de esa fábrica los hombres,
bajos los ojos, baja la cabeza.
Allí está el Tormes con su cielo alto,
niños por las orillas entre escombros
donde escarban gallinas. Mira, mira:
ve cómo ya, aun con muescas y clavijas,
con ceños y asperezas,
van fluyendo las cosas. Mana, fuente
de rica vena, mi mirada, mi única
salvación, sella, graba,
como en un árbol los enamorados,
la locura armoniosa de la vida
en tus veloces aguas pasajeras.

II

La misteriosa juventud constante
de lo que existe, su maravillosa
eternidad, hoy llaman
con sus nudillos muy heridos a esta
pupila prisionera. Hacía tiempo
(qué bien sé ahora el porqué) me era lo mismo
ver flor que llaga, cepo que caricia;

without being able to inhabit them.
How dark a gaze
at things so clear. Look, look:
there smoke rises, men begin to leave
the factory,
eyes down, heads bowed.
There's the Tormes River with its towering sky,
children on its banks in rubble
where chickens scratch. Look, look:
see how already, even with pegs and slots,
frowns and roughness,
things stream past. Flow,
bountiful fountain, my gaze,
my only salvation; stamp, engrave
as lovers do on trees,
the harmonious madness of life
in your swiftly flowing waters.

11

The mysterious unfailing youth
of all that exists, its marvelous
eternity, knock today with bruised knuckles
on these captive eyes. For a long time
(how well I know the reason now) it was all the same
if I saw flowers or a wound, traps or a caress,
but this evening has bared

pero esta tarde ha puesto al descubierto
mi soledad y miro
con mirada distinta. Compañeros
falsos y taciturnos,
cebados de consignas, si tan ricos
de propaganda, de canción tan pobres;
yo mismo, que fallé, tantas ciudades
con ese medallón de barro seco
de la codicia, tanto
pueblo rapaz al que a mi pesar quiero
me fueron, a hurtadillas,
haciendo mal de ojo y yo seguía
entre los sucios guiños, esperando
un momento. Éste de hoy. Tiembla en el aire
la última luz. Es la hora
en que nuestra mirada
se agracia y se adoncella.
La hora en que, al fin, con toda
la vergüenza en la cara, miro y cambio
mi vida entera por una mirada,
esa que ahora está lejos,
la única que me sirve, por la sola
cosa por la que quiero estos dos ojos:
esa mirada que no tiene dueño.

my loneliness, and I see with
a different gaze. False, diffident
friends full of slogans, rich
in propaganda but not in song,
I myself who failed, so many cities'
coats of arms, shaped from the clay
of avarice, so many covetous
people, who in spite of myself I love,
hexing me on the sly, and I stayed
there among their nasty winks, waiting for
the moment. This one today. The last light
trembles in the air. It's the hour
when our gaze turns
winsome and virginal.
The hour when at last,
face radiating shame,
I look and exchange
my whole life for a gaze,
the one now far away,
the only one that will do,
the only thing
I need these two eyes for:
the gaze that no one owns.

CÁSCARAS

I

E L nombre de las cosas que es mentira
y es caridad, el traje
que cubre el cuerpo amado
para que no muramos por la calle
ante él, las cuatro copas
que nos alegran al entrar en esos
edificios donde hay sangre y hay llanto,
hay vino y carcajadas,
el precinto y los cascos,
la cautela del sobre que protege
traición o amor, dinero o trampa,
la inmensa cicatriz que oculta la honda herida,
son nuestro ruin amparo.
Los sindicatos, las cooperativas,
los montepíos, los concursos;
ese prieto vendaje
de la costumbre, que nos tapa el ojo
para que no ceguemos,
la vana golosina de un día y otro día
templándonos la boca
para que el diente no busque la pulpa
fatal, son un engaño
venenoso y piadoso. Centinelas
vigilan. Nunca, nunca

HUSKS

I

T H E names of things that are falsehood
and charity, the clothes
that cover a beloved body
so we won't fall dead in the street
when we come face to face, the four drinks
that give us joy when we enter
those places of blood and wailing,
wine and raucous laughter,
legal seals and empty bottles,
furtive envelopes that hide
treachery or love, money or a trap,
the immense scar hiding a deep wound—
these are our ruthless protection.
The unions, the cooperatives,
the pension plans, the public bids,
that tight bandage
of custom that covers our eyes
so we won't go blind,
the useless candy of one day and another
sweetening our mouths
so no tooth will seek the fated flesh—
all are venomous, pious deceptions.
Sentries stand watch. They will never
give the password
to the terrible munitions, to the truth that kills.

darán la contraseña que conduce
a la terrible munición, a la verdad que mata.

II

Entre la empresa, el empresario, entre
prosperidad y goce,
entre un error prometedor y otra
ciencia a destiempo,
con el duro consuelo
de la palabra, que termina en burla
o en provecho o defensa,
o en viento
enerizo, o en pura
mutilación, no en canto;
entre gente que sólo
es muchedumbre, no
pueblo, ¿dónde
la oportunidad del amor,
de la contemplación libre o, al menos,
de la honda tristeza, del dolor verdadero?
La cáscara y la máscara,
los cuarteles, los foros y los claustros,
diplomas y patentes, halos, galas,
las más burdas mentiras:
la de la libertad mientras se dobla
la vigilancia,
¿han de dar vida a tanta
juventud macerada, tanta fe corrompida?

II

Between the business and the businessman,
between prosperity and pleasure,
between a promising error and
another outdated bit of wisdom,
with the harsh consolation
of words that end in mockery
or benefit or defense,
or in a January
wind or in plain
mutilation, but never in song;
among folk that are only a crowd
and never a people,
where is the chance for love,
for pure contemplation, or at least
profound sadness, genuine sorrow?
The husks and masks,
the barracks, the forums and cloisters,
the diplomas and patents, halos, galas,
and liberty —the clumsiest of lies—
while they double the watch,
can these instill life in so much
youth gone soft, so much corrupt faith?

Pero tú quema, quema
todas las cartas, todos los retratos,
los pajares del tiempo, la avena de la infancia.
El más seco terreno
es el de la renuncia. Quién pudiera
modelar con la lluvia esta de junio
un rostro, dices. Calla
y persevera aunque
ese rostro sea lluvia,
muerde la dura cáscara,
muerde aunque nunca llegues
hasta la celda donde cuaja el fruto.

But you, burn, burn
all the letters, all the photographs,
the haylofts of time, the oats of infancy.
The driest terrain
is that of renunciation. If one could
only model a face from this June rain,
you say. Be still and persevere
even though that face be rain;
bite the tough husk,
bite although you never reach
the cell where the fruit matures.

I

ARRODILLADO sobre
tantos días perdidos
contemplo hoy mi trabajo como a esa
ciudad lejana, a campo
abierto.
Y tú me culpas de ello
corazón, duro amo.
Que recuerde y olvide
que aligere y que cante
para pasar el tiempo,
para perder el miedo;
que tantos años vayan de vacío
por si nos llega algo
que cobije a los hombres.
Como siempre, ¿eso quieres?
En manada, no astutos
sino desconfiados,
unas veces altivos
otras menesterosos, por inercia
e ignorancia, en los brazos
del rencor, con la honra
de su ajo crudo y de su vino puro,
tú recuerda, recuerda
cuánto en su compañía
ganamos y perdimos.

IN WOLF COUNTRY

I

KNEELING down
on so many lost days,
I consider my work
as if it were that faraway city
on the empty plains.
And you blame me for this,
my heart, taskmaster.
Am I to remember and forget,
be cheerful and sing
to pass the time,
to quiet my fear,
to let so many years go by
in the hope of finding
something to shelter us?
As always, is that what you want?
Herded together, not cunning
but suspicious,
sometimes haughty,
and at others destitute from inertia
and ignorance, in the arms
of bitterness, with the honor
of raw garlic and pure wine.
Remember, just remember
how much we won
and lost in their company.

¿Cómo podrás ahora
acompasar deber
con alegría, dicha
con dinero? Mas sigue.
No hay que buscar ningún
beneficio.
Lejos están aquellas
mañanas.

Las mañanas aquellas pobres de vestuario
como la muerte, llenas
de rodillas beatas y de manos
del marfil de la envidia y de unos dientes
muy blancos y cobardes,
de conejo. Esas calles
de hundida proa con costumbre añosa
de señera pobreza,
de raída arrogancia, como cuñas
que sostienen tan sólo
una carcoma irremediable. Y notas
de sociedad, linaje, favor público,
de terciopelo y pana, caqui y dril,
donde la adulación color lagarto
junto con la avaricia olor a incienso
me eran como enemigos
de nacimiento. Aquellas
mañanas con su fuerte
luz de meseta, tan consoladora.
Aquellas niñas que iban al colegio
de ojos castaños casi todas ellas,

How can you balance now
duty and joy, happiness
and money? Keep going.
It's pointless to look
for any profit.
Those mornings
were long ago.

Those mornings, poorly dressed
like death, with
prayer-stiff knees, envious
ivory hands and rabbits'
white cowardly teeth. Those sunken-
prowed streets with ancient customs
of titled poverty, threadbare arrogance,
were wedges that only shored up
the termites' implacable work.
Society notices, family trees, public renown,
velvet and corduroy, khaki and drill,
where lizard-colored flattery,
together with avarice that smelled of incense,
were my enemies since I was born.
Those mornings
with their harsh highland
light that comforted us.
Those little girls off to school,
almost all with hazel eyes,
and still not far from sleep
but already close to joy. Yes, and those men

aún no lejos del sueño y ya muy cerca
de la alegría. Sí, y aquellos hombres
en los que confié, tan sólo ávidos
de municiones y de víveres...

A veces, sin embargo, en esas tierras
floreció la amistad. Y muchas veces
hasta el amor. Doy gracias.

11

Erguido sobre
tantos días alegres,
sigo la marcha. No podré habitarte,
ciudad cercana. Siempre seré huésped,
nunca vecino.
Ahora ya el sol tramonta. De esos cerros
baja un olor que es frío aquí en el llano.
El color oro mate poco a poco
se hace bruñida plata. Cae la noche.

No me importó otras veces
la alta noche,
recordadlo. Sé que era lamentable
el trato aquel, el hueco
repertorio de gestos
desvencijados
sobre cuerpos de vario
surtido y con tan poca

I trusted who only
wanted weapons and rations...

Even so, hereabouts
there was friendship and often
even love. For this I give thanks.

II

Standing upright on
so many joyful days
I keep going. I can't settle here,
nearby city. I'll always be a visitor,
never a neighbor.
Now the mountains hide the sun. A smell
descends that is cold here below.
A dull gold color turns little by little
to burnished silver. Night comes on.

Remember this:
I never minded darkest night.
I know my behavior
was shameful, an empty
repertoire of caved-in
gestures on a varied choice
of bodies with so little grace.
And the missals

gracia para actuar. Y los misales
y las iglesias parroquiales,
y la sotana y la badana, hombres
con diminutos ojos triangulares
como los de la abeja,
legitimando oficialmente el fraude,
la perfidia, y haciendo
la vida negociable; las mujeres
de honor pulimentado, liquidadas
por cese o por derribo,
su mocedad y su frescura
cristalizadas en
ansiedad, rutina
vitalicia, encogiendo
como algodón. Sí, sí, la vieja historia.
Como en la vieja historia oí aquellas
palabras a alta noche, con alcohol,
o de piel de gamuza
o bien correosas, córneas, nunca humanas.
Vi la decrepitud, el mimbre negro.
Oí que eran dolorosas las campanas
a las claras del alba.

Es hora muy tardía
mas quiero entrar en la ciudad. Y sigo.
Va a amanecer. ¿Dónde hallaré vivienda?

and parochial churches,
the black robes and limber canes,
men with tiny triangular eyes like bees,
officially sanctioning fraud,
disloyalty, life up for sale;
women with burnished honor,
out of business,
let go or torn down,
their youth and their freshness
crystallized in anxiety, in life-long
routine, shriveling
like cotton cloth. Yes, yes, the old story.
As in the old stories at midnight
after liters of wine, I heard words
of soft chamois, or stiff, or opaque, never human.
I saw decrepitude, blackened cane,
understood how the church bells
caused grief at first light.

It's late,
I want to enter the city. I go on.
It's almost morning. Where will I find shelter?

EUGENIO DE LUELMO

Que vivió y murió junto al Duero

I

CUANDO amanece alguien con gracia de tan sencillas
como a su lado son las cosas, casi
parecen nuevas, casi
sentimos el castigo, el miedo oscuro
de poseer. Para esa
propagación inmensa del que ama
floja es la sangre nuestra. La eficacia de este hombre,
sin ensayo, el negocio
del mar que eran sus gestos ola a ola,
flor y fruto a la vez, y muerte y nacimiento
al mismo tiempo, y ese gran peligro
de su ternura, de su modo de ir
por las calles nos daban
la única justicia: la alegría.
Como quien fuma al pie
de un polvorín sin darse cuenta íbamos con él
y como era tan fácil
de invitar no veíamos
que besaba al beber y que al hacerle trampas
en el tute, más en el mus, jugaba
de verdad, con sus cartas
sin marca. Él, cuyo oficio sin horario
era la compañía, ¿cómo iba

EUGENIO DE LUELMO

Who lived and died by the Duero River

I

W H E N someone is born with a special gift,
so that things in their presence seem simple, new,
we almost feel the punishment, the dark fear
of possession. For their unending gift of love
our blood is thin. The bounty of this unpracticed
man, with gestures like the working of the sea,
wave after wave, at once flower and fruit,
death and birth together,
and the great danger of his tenderness,
his way of walking our streets,
gave us our only justice: joy.
Like someone smoking unaware
by a powder keg, we kept his company,
and because it was so easy
to buy him a drink we never saw
how he kissed as he drank,
and when we cheated him at cards,
at *Tute*, even more at *Mus*,
we never noticed how he played fair,
his cards unmarked. This man, whose hourless
labor was company, how could he know
his Duero River is a bad neighbor?

a saber que su Duero
es mal vecino?

II

Caminos por ventilar
que oreó con su asma,
son de tambores del que él hizo arrullo
siendo de guerra, leyes que dividían
a tajo hombre por hombre
de las que él hizo injertos para poblar su agrio
vacío no con saña,
menos con propaganda,
sino con lo más fértil, su llaneza,
todo ardía en el horno de sus setenta y dos años.
Allí todo era llama
siempre atizada, incendio sin cenizas
desde el sueldo hasta el hijo,
desde las canas hasta la ronquera,
desde la pana al alma. Como alondra
se agachaba al andar y se le abría un poco
el compás de las piernas, con el aire
del que ha cargado mucho (tan distinto
del que monta a caballo o del marino).
Apagada la oreja,
oliendo a cal, a arena, a vino, a sebo,
iba sin despedida:
todo él era retorno.
Esa velocidad conquistadora

When paths needed airing
he cleared them with his asthma,
he made drum-raps sound like cooing
although they meant war. From laws that severed
one man from another, he made grafts
to reforest the law's bitter omissions,
not with rancor, much less with propaganda,
but with what was most fertile—his naturalness.
Everything burned in the oven of his seventy-two years.
There everything was a flame
that was always banked,
a fire without ash from his wages to his son,
from his gray hair to his hoarseness,
from his corduroy to his soul. Like the lark
he crouched as he walked, his legs bowed out
with the air of a carrier of heavy loads
(so different from the bowed legs
of horsemen and sailors).
Nearly hard of hearing,
smelling of whitewash, sand, wine, suet,
he would go off without goodbye—
he was all return.
The conquering rapidity of his life,
his lizard blood, eagle's blood, hound's blood,

de su vida, su sangre
de lagartija, de águila y de perro,
se nos metían en el cuerpo como
música caminera. Ciegos para el misterio
y, por lo tanto, tuertos
para lo real, ricos sólo de imágenes
y sólo de recuerdos, ¿cómo vamos ahora
a celebrar lo que es suceso puro,
noticia sin historia, trabajo que es hazaña?

III

No bajo la cabeza,
Eugenio, aunque yo bien sé que ahora
no me conocerían ni aun en casa.
La muerte no es un río, como el Duero,
ni tampoco es un mar. Como el amor, el mar
siempre acaba entre cuatro
paredes. Y tú, Eugenio, por mil cauces
sin crecida o sequía,
sin puentes, sin mujeres
lavando ropa, ¿en qué aguas
te has metido?
Pero tú no reflejas, como el agua;
como tierra, posees.
Y el hilván de estas calles
de tu barriada al par del río,
y las sobadas briscas,
y el dar la mano sin dar ya verano

ran through our veins like
walk-along music. Blind to the mystery
and therefore half seeing
what's real, rich only in images
and memories, how can we celebrate now
what is pure event, news without history,
work that's a victory?

III

I don't bow my head,
Eugenio, although I know
I'd be a stranger at home.
Death isn't a river like the Duero,
and it isn't the sea. Like love
the sea always ends between four walls.
And you, Eugenio, down countless streambeds
without flood or drought,
without bridges or washerwomen,
into what deep water did you go?
But you don't reflect like water,
like the earth you possess.
And the threading streets
of your neighborhood by the river,
your grimy deck of cards,
your shaking of hands "with no summer around,"
nothing real, no life by the cartload,

ni realidad, ni vida
a mansalva, y la lengua
ya tonta de decir «adiós», «adiós»,
y el sol ladrón y huido,
y esas torres de húmeda
pólvora, de calibre
perdido, y yo con este aire de primero de junio
que hace ruido en mi pecho,
y los amigos… Mucho,
en poco tiempo mucho ha terminado.
Ya cuesta arriba o cuesta abajo,
hacia la plaza o hacia tu taller,
todo nos mira ahora
de soslayo, nos coge
fuera de sitio.
Nos da como vergüenza
vivir, nos da vergüenza
respirar, ver lo hermosa
que cae la tarde. Pero
por el ojo de todas las cerraduras del mundo
pasa tu llave y abre
familiar, luminosa,
y así entramos en casa
como aquel que regresa de una cita cumplida.

your tongue thick with saying "So long, so long."
And that thieving, runaway sun,
and those towers with their gunpowder damp,
their canons spiked, and me with this air
of the first of June rattling in my chest,
and our friends... Much
in a short time, so much has ended.
Whether uphill or down,
to the town square or your workshop,
now everything stares at us
from the corner of an eye,
and catches us out of place.
We're almost ashamed to live,
ashamed to breathe,
to watch the lovely afternoon
fade away. But your key
fits every lock in the world,
and luminous, familiar it opens them,
and so we enter our houses,
like someone returning
from an appointment they'd kept.

NUNCA a tientas, así, como ahora, entra
por este barrio. Así, así, sin limosna,
sin tregua, entra, acorrala,
mete tu cruda forja
por estas casas. De una vez baja, abre
y cicatriza esta honda
miseria. Baja ahora que no hay nadie,
noche mía, no alejes, no recojas
tu infinito latir ávido. Acaba
ya de cernirte, acosa
de una vez a esta presa a la que nadie
quiere valer. Sólo oiga,
noche mía, después de tantos años,
el son voraz de tu horda luminosa
saqueando hasta el fondo
tanta orfandad, la agria pobreza bronca
de este bloque en silencio que está casi
en el campo y aloja
viva siembra vibrante. Desmantele
tu luz nuestra injusticia y nos la ponga
al aire, y la descarne,
y la sacuda, y la haga pegajosa
como esta tierra, y que nos demos cuenta
de que está aquí, a dos pasos. Protectora
nunca, sí con audacia.
Acusa. Y que la casta,
la hombría de alta cal, los sueños, la obra,

NIGHT IN OUR NEIGHBORHOOD

E N T E R this neighborhood
as now, never with caution.
Thus, thus, without alms,
without truce, enter, corral,
force your cruel forge
on these houses. Come down,
all at once, open and heal this deep misery.
Come down now when there is no one,
oh night, don't go off, don't take back
your infinite, passionate throbbing. Stop
hovering near, attack all at once this
prey for whom no one will speak.
Only hear, oh night, after so many years,
the voracious sound of your radiant horde,
plundering completely all this orphanhood,
the coarse bitter poverty of this silent
block, almost touching the fields
and enfolding vibrant seeds. Let your light
tear down our injustice and hang it out,
flay it and shake it, make it sticky
like this earth, and may we realize
that it's here just a few steps away.
Never protecting, always audacious.
Accuse. And may the lineage,
the honesty of prime whitewash,
the dreams, the work, the bare frame
of life turn tense and angry.

el armazón desnudo de la vida
se crispen.

Y estás sola,
tú, noche, enloquecida de justicia,
anonadada de misericordia,
sobre este barrio trémulo al que nadie
vendrá porque es la historia
de todos, pero al que tú siempre, en andas
y en volandas,
llevas, y traes, y hieres, y enamoras
sin que nadie lo sepa,
sin que nadie oiga el ruido
de tus inmensos pulsos, que desbordan.

And you're alone,
oh night, maddened with justice,
worn down by pity,
over this tremulous neighborhood
to which no one will come
because it's the story of everyone,
but that you always hold high,
take away and bring back,
wound and make fall in love,
without anyone knowing,
without anyone hearing the noise
of your enormous pulsating that overwhelms.

II

MIRO la espuma, su delicadeza
que es tan distinta a la de la ceniza.
Como quien mira una sonrisa, aquella
por la que da su vida y le es fatiga
y amparo, miro ahora la modesta
espuma. Es el momento bronco y bello
del uso, el roce, el acto de la entrega
creándola. El dolor encarcelado
del mar se salva en fibra tan ligera;
bajo la quilla, frente al dique, donde
existe amor surcado, como en tierra
la flor, nace la espuma. Y es en ella
donde rompe la muerte, en su madeja
donde el mar cobra ser como en la cima
de su pasión el hombre es hombre, fuera
de otros negocios: en su leche viva.
A este pretil, brocal de la materia
que es manantial, no desembocadura,
me asomo ahora cuando la marea
sube, y allí naufrago, allí me ahogo
muy silenciosamente, con entera
aceptación, ileso, renovado
en las espumas imperecederas.

FOAM

I look at the foam, at its delicacy,
so different from the airiness of ashes.
Like someone watching a smile, the one
they give their life for, both a burden
and a comfort, I look now at the humble
foam. This is the rough, beautiful moment
of its use, its contact, the act of offering
that creates it. The imprisoned sorrow of the sea
is saved in this weightless fiber; under keels,
against piers, where furrowed love exists,
as with flowers ashore, this foam is born.
And here death breaks, in its skein where the sea
becomes sea, as man is man at the height
of his passion, beyond other tasks, in his living
semen. At this rail, this well-side of matter,
a fresh spring and not the mouth of a river,
I lean out now as the tide is rising
and there I drown, silently founder there,
with complete acceptance, unscathed,
renewed in the imperishable foam.

VIENTO DE PRIMAVERA

A Winifred Grillet

N I aun el cuerpo resiste
tanta resurrección y busca abrigo
ante este viento que ya templa y trae
olor y nueva intimidad. Ya cuanto
fue hambre ahora es sustento. Y se aligera
la vida, y un destello generoso
vibra por nuestras calles. Pero sigue
turbia nuestra retina y la saliva
seca, y los pies van a la desbandada,
como siempre. Y entonces,
esta presión fogosa que nos trae
el cuerpo aún frágil de la primavera,
ronda en torno al invierno
de nuestro corazón, buscando un sitio
por donde entrar en él. Y aquí, a la vuelta
de la esquina, al acecho,
en feraz merodeo,
nos ventea la ropa,
nos orea el trabajo,
barre la casa, engrasa nuestras puertas
duras de oscura cerrazón, las abre
a no sé qué hospitalidad hermosa
y nos desborda y, aunque
nunca nos demos cuenta
de tanta juventud, de lleno en lleno

SPRING WIND

For Winifred Grillet

NOT even the body can withstand
so much resurrection, and it seeks shelter
from this wind that eases now, and brings
smells and a new intimacy. Now all
that was hunger is nourishment. And life
lightens, and a generous sparkling
pulses in our streets. But our sight
is still cloudy, our spittle dry
and our feet go hurrying off,
as always. And then
this sultry pressure that the still-
fragile body of spring brings,
circles around the winter
of our hearts, searching for a point
of entry. And waiting here,
just around the corner,
successfully marauding,
it blows at our clothing,
dries out our labor,
sweeps our houses, eases our doors
shut dark and tight, and opens them
to I don't know what pleasant hospitality,
overwhelms us, and even if we're never
aware of so much youth, it rushes
us along. Yes, with the sun

nos arrasa. Sí, a poco
del sol salido, un viento ya gustoso,
sereno de simiente, sopló en torno
de nuestra sequedad, de la injusticia
de nuestros años, alentó para algo
más hermoso que tanta
desconfianza y tanto desaliento,
más valiente que nuestro
miedo a su honda rebelión, a su alta
resurrección. Y ahora
yo, que perdí mi libertad por todo,
quiero oír cómo el pobre
ruido de nuestro pulso se va a rastras
tras el cálido son de esta alianza
y ambos hacen la música
arrolladora, sin compás, a sordas,
por la que sé que llegará algún día,
quizá en medio de enero, en el que todos
sepamos el porqué del nombre: «viento
de primavera».

just risen a delicious wind
carrying seedlings, blew around
our dryness, the injustice
of our years, inspired us to something
more lovely than all
our wariness, all our despair,
something braver than our fear
of its sweeping rebellion,
its fierce resurrection. And now
I, who lost so much liberty,
want to hear the faint noise
of our pulse as it edges after
the warm sound of this alliance,
and together they make
an overwhelming, rhythm-less,
soundless music, by which I know
that one day,
perhaps in mid-January,
the time will come
when we'll all know the why of its name:
"Spring Wind."

N O olvida. No se aleja
este granuja astuto
de nuestra vida. Siempre
de prestado, sin rumbo,
como cualquiera, aquí anda,
se lava aquí, tozudo,
entre nuestros zapatos.
¿Qué busca en nuestro oscuro
vivir? ¿Qué amor encuentra
en nuestro pan tan duro?
Ya dio al aire a los muertos
este gorrión que pudo
volar pero aquí sigue,
aquí abajo, seguro,
metiendo en su pechuga
todo el polvo del mundo.

SPARROW

IT's constant. This sly
creature stays close
to our lives. Always
on loan, without direction,
like most of us it scratches here,
bathes itself here, stubbornly,
between our shoes.
What does it expect to find
in our dark lives? What love
in our crusts of bread?
This sparrow has already
tossed death to the four winds.
It could have flown off
but remained here,
here below, confident,
dusting its breast
in all the dust of the world.

DESDE el autobús, lleno
de labriegos, de curas y de gallos,
al llegar a Palencia,
veo a ese hombre.
Comienza a llover fuerte, casi arrecia
y no le va a dar tiempo
a refugiarse en la ciudad. Y corre
como quien asesina. Y no comprende
el castigo del agua, su sencilla
servidumbre; tan sólo estar a salvo
es lo que quiere. Por eso no sabe
que le crece como un renuevo fértil
en su respiración acelerada,
que es cebo vivo, amor ya sin remedio,
cantera rica. Y, ante la sorpresa
de tal fecundidad,
se atropella y recela;
siente, muy en lo oscuro, que está limpio
para siempre pero él no lo resiste;
y mira, y busca, y huye,
y, al llegar a cubierto,
entra mojado y libre, y se cobija,
y respira tranquilo en su ignorancia
al ver cómo su ropa
poco a poco se seca.

RAIN AND GRACE

FROM the bus, full
of farm hands, priests and roosters,
coming into Palencia,
I see this man.
It starts to rain, then harder
and he won't have time
to take shelter in the city. And he runs
like a murderer. And doesn't understand
the rain's punishment, its selfless
servitude; just to be out of it
is what he wants. That's why he doesn't
know a ripe bud's growing
in his quickened breath,
that it's live bait, a love he can't put down,
a rich quarry. And taken aback
by this fruitfulness
he stumbles and dodges;
he feels, darkly within, that he's clean
forever, but he can't stand it
and he stares, hunts and runs,
and getting to cover,
goes in wet and free, huddles down
and breathes easy in his unknowing,
as he sees how his clothes
dry out little by little.

GIRASOL

ESTA cara bonita,
este regazo que fue flor y queda
tan pronto encinta y yo lo quiero, y ahora
me lo arrimo, y me entra
su luminosa rotación sencilla,
su danza que es cosecha,
por el alma esta tarde
de septiembre, de buena
ventura porque ahora tú, valiente
girasol de tan ciega
mirada, tú me hacías mucha falta
con tu postura de perdón tras esa
campaña soleada
de altanería, a tierra
la cabeza, vencida
por tanto grano, tan loca empresa.

SUNFLOWER

THIS pretty face,
this lap that was a flower
and is suddenly pregnant,
and I love it and now hold it close,
and its simple, luminous rotation,
its dance that's a harvest,
enter my soul this September
noon; and I am fortunate now
because brave, sightless
sunflower, I needed you so,
with your gesture of forgiveness,
after that sunny campaign
of haughtiness, your head
hanging down, overwhelmed
by the mad enterprise
of all those seeds.

LA luz entusiasmada de conquista
pierde confianza ahora,
trémula de impotencia y no se sabe
si es de tierra o de cielo. Se despoja
de su íntima ternura
y se retira lenta. ¿Qué limosna
sin regocijo? ¿Qué reposo seco
nos trae la tarde? ¿Qué misericordia
deja este sol de un grana desvaído?
¿Quién nos habló de la honda
piedad del cielo? Aún quedan
restos de la audaz forja
de la luz pero pocas
nuevas nos vienen de la vida: un ruido,
algún olor mal amasado, esta hosca
serenidad de puesta, cuando
lejos están los campos y aún más lejos
el fuego del hogar, y esta derrota
nuestra por cobardía o arrogancia,
por inercia o por gloria
como la de esta luz ya sin justicia
ni rebelión, ni aurora.

FADED SUNSET

THE light, excited by conquest,
loses confidence now,
trembling with impotence. And we wonder
if it belongs to the earth or sky. It shrugs
off its intimate tenderness
and slowly withdraws. What alms given
without happiness? What sudden rest
does this evening bring? What compassion
is there in this faded reddish light?
Who spoke to us of the sky's
profound pity? Something still remains
of the awesome forge of light
but little news of life: a sound,
a partly-blended smell, the brusque
calm of sunset, when the fields are far off
and the hearth fires even farther,
and our defeat, from cowardice
or arrogance, inertia or glory—
like that of this light,
now without justice,
rebellion or dawn.

DINERO

¿VENDERÉ mis palabras hoy que carezco de
utilidad, de ingresos, hoy que nadie me fía?
Necesito dinero para el amor, pobreza
para amar. Y el precio de un recuerdo, la subasta
de un vicio, el inventario de un deseo,
dan valor, no virtud, a mis necesidades,
amplio vocabulario a mis torpezas,
licencia a mi caliza
soledad. Porque el dinero, a veces, es el propio
sueño, es la misma
vida. Y su triunfo, su monopolio, da fervor,
cambio, imaginación, quita vejez y abre
ceños y multiplica los amigos,
y alza faldas y es miel
cristalizando luz, calor. No plaga, lepra
como hoy; alegría,
no frivolidad; ley,
no impunidad. ¿Voy a vender, entonces,
estas palabras? Rico de tanta pérdida,
sin maniobras, sin bolsa, aun sin tentación
y aun sin ruina dorada, ¿a qué la madriguera
de estas palabras que si dan aliento
no dan dinero? ¿Prometen pan o armas?
¿O bien, como un balance mal urdido,
intentan ordenar un tiempo de carestía,
dar sentido a una vida: propiedad o desahucio?

MONEY

SHALL I sell these words today
when I'm of no use, without income,
with no one to give me credit?
I need money for love, poverty
in order to love. And the price of a memory,
the auction of a vice, the inventory of a desire
lend boldness, not virtue, to my needs,
a generous vocabulary to my confusion,
consent to my quicklime solitude.
Because sometimes money is the stuff
of dreams, is life itself.
And its triumph, its monopoly, lends
fervor, change, imagination; it erases old age
and smooths brows, multiplies friends,
raises skirts and is honey
crystallizing light, warmth. Not plague,
leprosy as today; joy,
not frivolity; law,
not impunity. Then, will I sell these words?
Rich from so many losses,
with no elbowroom, purse, or temptation,
or even false gold, of what use is this mare's nest
of words that although it does bring relief
won't earn me any money? A promise of bread
or weapons? Or like unbalanced books,
will it redress this time of privation,
give life a meaning: ownership or foreclosure?

Y O quiero ver qué arrugas
oculta esta doncella
máscara. Qué ruin tiña,
qué feroz epidemia
cela el rostro inocente
de cada copo. Escenas
sin vanidad se cubren
con andamiajes, trémulas
escayolas, molduras
de un instante. Es la feria
de la mentira: ahora
es mediodía en plena
noche, y se cicatriza
la eterna herida abierta
de la tierra y las casas
lucen con la cal nueva
que revoca sus pobres
fachadas verdaderas.

La nieve, tan querida
otro tiempo, nos ciega,
no da luz. Copo a copo,
como ladrón, recela
al caer. Cae temblando,
cae sin herirse apenas
con nuestras cosas diarias.
Tan sin dolor, su entrega

SNOWFALL AT NIGHT

I want to see what wrinkles
this virginal mask covers.
What dreadful blemish,
what fierce epidemic
the innocent face
of every snowflake hides. Modest
scenes hidden by scaffoldings,
tremulous plastering,
momentary moldings. It's a festival
of lies: it's midday now
in the middle of the night,
and earth's eternal open wound
is healed, and houses glisten
as fresh whitewash
covers their sad true facades.

The snow I loved to watch before
blinds us, gives no light.
Snowflake after snowflake, thief-
like, evasive, falls trembling,
almost not wounding itself
on our everyday things.
So painless that its gift
of self is cruelty. It falls,

es crueldad. Cae, cae,
hostil al canto, lenta,
bien domada, bien dócil,
como sujeta a riendas
que nunca se aventuran
a conquistar. No riega
sino sofoca, ahoga
dando no amor, paciencia.

Y borró los caminos.
Y tú dices: «despierta,
que amanece». (Y es noche
muy noche.) Dices: «cierra,
que entra sol». Y no quiero
perder de nuevo ante esta
nevada. No, no quiero
mentirte otra vez. Tengo
que alzarle la careta
a este rostro enemigo
que me finge a mi puerta
la inocencia que vuelve
y el pie que deja huella.

falls slowly, wary of edges,
as though well-broken, docile,
checked by reins it never thinks
to chafe at. It doesn't refresh,
it suffocates; it drowns us
not with love but patience.

And it erased all the paths.
And you say: "Wake up,
it's morning." (But still it's
night, the middle of the night.)
And you say: "Close the blinds,
you're letting in the sun."
And I don't want to lose
to this snowfall again. No,
I don't want to lie to you again.
I must unmask this enemy face
that feigns at my door
the return of innocence
and footsteps in the snow.

FRENTE AL MAR

Desde « Las Mayoas », Ibiza
A Carlos Bousoño

TRANSPARENTE quietud. Frente a la tierra
rojiza, desecada hasta la entraña,
con aridez que es ya calcinación,
se abre el Mediterráneo. Hay pino bajo,
sabinas, pitas, y crece el tomillo
y el fiel romero tan austeramente
que apenas huelen si no es a salitre.
Quema la tramontana. Cae la tarde.
Verdad de sumisión, de entrega, de
destronamientos, desmoronamientos
frente al mar azul puro que en la orilla
se hace verde esmeralda. Vieja y nueva
erosión. Placas, láminas, cornisas,
acantilados y escolleras, ágil
bisel, estría, lucidez de roca
de milenaria permanencia. Aquí
la verdad de la piedra, nunca muda
sino en interna reverberación,
en estremecimiento de cosecha
perenne dando su seguro oficio,
su secreta ternura sobria junto
al mar que es demasiada criatura,
demasiada hermosura para el hombre.
Antiguo mar latino que hoy no canta,

MEDITERRANEAN SEA

At «Las Mayoas,» Ibiza
For Carlos Bousoño

T R A N S P A R E N T calm. By this ochre
shore, parched to the very bone,
drier than calcinated lime,
lies the Mediterranean Sea.
There are stunted pines,
low spreading juniper, agave;
faithful rosemary and thyme
whose growth is so austere
they only smell of clinging brine.
North Wind afire. The setting sun.
True submission, true surrender,
loss of thrones, dynastic ruination,
against a pure blue sea that
once inshore turns emerald green.
Old and new erosion. Caps, layers,
cornices, cliffs and rocky shelves,
grooves, sharp incisions, clarity of rock,
a permanence measured in eons.
This is the truth of stone, never
silent but with an inner resonance
that wills its own design of endless
harvests; its chaste, secret tenderness
by a sea that's much too young,
too beautiful for mankind.

dice apenas, susurra, prisionero
de su implacable poderío, con
pulsación de sofoco, sin oleaje,
casi en silencio de clarividencia
mientras el cielo se oscurece y llega,
maciza y seca, la última ocasión
para amar. Entre piedras y entre espumas,
¿qué es rendición y qué supremacía?
¿Qué nos serena, qué nos atormenta:
el mar terso o la tierra desolada?

Ancient Latin sea that today
doesn't sing, that barely speaks,
although it whispers, prisoner
of its own relentless power,
its measured breathlessness,
its stillness, a near visionary
silence, as the sky darkens and
it's our final chance, solid, dry,
to make love. With these pebbles
and this foam, what is surrender,
what is victory? What will soothe us,
what torment us: the lustrous
sea or the desolate land?

COMO por estos sitios
tan sano aire no hay pero no vengo
a curarme de nada.
Vengo a saber qué hazaña
vibra en la luz, qué rebelión oscura
nos arrasa hoy la vida.
Aquí ya no hay banderas,
ni murallas, ni torres, como si ahora
pudiera todo resistir el ímpetu
de la tierra, el saqueo
del cielo. Y se nos barre
la vista, es nuestro cuerpo
mercado franco, nuestra voz vivienda
y el amor y los años
puertas para uno y para mil que entrasen.
Sí, tan sin suelo siempre,
cuando hoy andamos por las viejas calles
el talón se nos tiñe
de uva nueva y oímos
desbordar bien sé qué aguas
el rumoroso cauce del oído.

Es la alianza: este aire
montaraz con tensión de compañía.
Y a saber qué distancia
hay de hombre a hombre, de una vida a otra,
qué planetaria dimensión separa

CITY ON THE HIGH PLAINS

NOWHERE is the air
this healthy but I'm not
here to be cured of anything.
I've come to learn what heroics
vibrate in this light,
what dark rebellion levels life today.
Here there are no more banners,
walls or towers, as though now
all could withstand this thrusting
of the earth, this sacking
by the sky. Our gaze is swept
clear, the body is an open market,
the voice a habitation and
our love and our years doors
for one, for a thousand, to enter by.
Yes, our heads are in the clouds,
but today as we walk these ancient streets
our heels stain grape-red,
and we hear the waters I know so well
flood the murmuring trough of our ears.

It's all alliance: this mountain
air with its heightened company.
And let's see what distance there is
from man to man, from life to life,
what planetary sweep separates

dos latidos, qué inmensa lejanía
hay entre dos miradas
o de la boca al beso.
¿Para qué tantos planos
sórdidos, de ciudades bien trazadas
junto a ríos, fundadas
en la separación, en el orgullo
roquero?
Jamás casas: barracas,
jamás calles: trincheras,
jamás jornal: soldada.
¿De qué han servido tanta
plaza fuerte, hondo foso, recia almena,
amurallado cerco?
El temor, la defensa,
el interés y la venganza, el odio,
la soledad: he aquí lo que nos hizo
vivir en vecindad, no en compañía.
Tal es la cruel escena
que nos dejaron por herencia. Entonces,
¿cómo fortificar aquí la vida
si ella es sólo alianza?

Heme ante tus murallas,
fronteriza ciudad a la que siempre
el cielo sin cesar desasosiega.
Vieja ambición que ahora
sólo admira el turista o el arqueólogo
o quien gusta de timbres y blasones.
Esto no es monumento

two heartbeats, what vast distance
there is between two glances
or between lips and a kiss.
Why so many rumpled plans
for cities meant to stand by rivers,
but founded on separation, rocky
pride? Never houses: barracks;
never streets: trenches;
never wages: pay.
Of what use were those
armed plazas, deep moats,
massive turrets, high
surrounding walls?
Fear, defensiveness,
self-interest, vengeance, hatred,
solitude: these are what made us live
not as neighbors but side by side.
That's the cruel setting
of our inheritance. But then
how can we ever fortify life
if here life is all alliance?

Here I am under your walls,
frontier city that the sky
has always made uneasy.
Ancient ambition that now
only tourists and archeologists
or lovers of crests
and shields admire.

nacional sino luz de alta planicie,
aire fresco que riega el pulmón árido
y lo ensancha y lo hace
total entrega renovada, patria
a campo abierto. Aquí no hay costas, mares,
norte ni sur; aquí todo es materia
de cosecha. Y si dentro
de poco llega la hora de la ida,
adiós al fuerte anillo
de aire y oro de alianza, adiós al cerro
que no es baluarte sino compañía,
adiós a tantos hombres
hasta hoy sin rescate. Porque todo
se rinde en derredor y no hay fronteras,
ni distancia, ni historia.
Sólo el voraz espacio y el relente de octubre
sobre estos altos campos
de nuestra tierra.

This is no national monument
but light of the high plains,
chill air to irrigate dry lungs,
swell them and make of them
a whole new offering,
a homeland of all outdoors.
Here are neither coasts nor seas,
north or south; here all
is the stuff of harvests. And if it's
soon time to leave,
farewell to this powerful alliance,
this wedding band of air and gold,
farewell to the mountain range
that isn't a palisade but company,
farewell to so many men
not ransomed until today. Because now
surrender is everywhere, and there
is no frontier, distance, or history.
Only voracious space and October's
morning chill on the high fields
of our homeland.

III

UN SUCESO

Bien est verté que j'ai amé
et ameroie voulentiers...

FRANÇOIS VILLON

TAL vez, valiendo lo que vale un día,
sea mejor que el de hoy acabe pronto.
La novedad de este suceso, de esta
muchacha casi niña pero de ojos
bien sazonados ya y de carne a punto
de miel, de andar menudo, con su moño
castaño claro, su tobillo hendido
tan armoniosamente, con su airoso
pecho que me deslumbra más que nada
la lengua... Y no hay remedio, y la hablo ronco
como la gaviota, a flor de labio
(de mi boca gastada), y me emociono
disimulando ciencia e inocencia
como quien no distingue un abalorio
de un diamante, y la hablo de detalles
de mi vida, y la voz se me va, y me oigo
y me persigo, muy desconfiado
de mi estudiada habilidad, y pongo
cuidado en el aliento, en la mirada
y en las manos, y casi me perdono
al sentir tan preciosa libertad
cerca de mí. Bien sé que esto no es sólo
tentación. Cómo renuncio a mi deseo

AN EVENT

It is true that I have loved
and will happily love again...
FRANÇOIS VILLON

PERHAPS since a day is worth so little
it's best if today were over soon.
The surprise of this meeting, of this
young girl, little more than a child,
but already with well-seasoned eyes and flesh
that's nearly honey, with short quick steps,
with pinned-up chestnut hair, her straight
delicate ankles and her pert breasts
that more than anything dazzle
my tongue... But there's no avoiding it,
and I speak to her hoarsely like
a seagull, but with winning words
(from my used-up mouth), and I am so moved,
hiding cleverness and innocence,
like someone who can't tell a bauble
from a diamond, that I tell her of parts
of my life and my voice runs on and I hear
myself and follow after, not trusting
my studied cunning, and I breathe
carefully, rein in looking and touching,
and almost forgive myself, now
that I feel such precious freedom
near. I know this isn't only

ahora. Me lastimo y me sonrojo
junto a esta muchacha a la que hoy amo,
a la que hoy pierdo, a la que muy pronto
voy a besar muy castamente sin que
sepa que en ese beso va un sollozo.

temptation. And how I forego
my desire. I pity myself and blush,
close to this young girl that today
I love, that today I lose, that soon
I will chastely kiss, without her
knowing that this kiss contains a sob.

CONMIGO tú no tengas
remordimiento, madre. Yo te doy lo único
que puedo darte ahora: si no amor,
sí reconciliación. Ya sé el fracaso,
la victoria que cabe
en un cuerpo. El caer, el arruinarse
de tantos años contra el pedernal
del dolor, el huir
con leyes a mansalva
que me daban razón, un cruel masaje
para alejarme de ti; historias
de dinero y de catres,
de alquileres sin tasa,
cuando todas mis horas eran horas de lobo,
cuando mi vida fue estar al acecho
de tu caída, de tu
herida, en la que puse,
si no el diente, tampoco
la lengua,
me dan hoy el tamaño
de mi pecado.

Sólo he crecido en esqueleto: mírame.
Asómate como antes
a la ventana. Tú no pienses nunca
en esa caña cruda que me irguió
hace dieciséis años. Tú ven, ven,

D O N ' T feel remorse
for me, Mother. I give you now
the only thing I can: if not love,
reconciliation. I know how much failure
and victory a body
can contain. The fall, the ruining
oneself for so many years
on the flint of pain, flight
despite a surfeit of laws
that proved me right, cruel favors
to separate me from you, stories
of money and makeshift beds,
of rentals without limit,
when wolfishly I lived the hours of my days,
when my life was devoted to stalking
your fall, your
wound, in which I sank
neither teeth nor
tongue,
today show me the measure
of my sin.

Only my skeleton has grown: look at me.
Come to the window
as before. Don't ever think of
the harsh cane that set me straight
now sixteen years ago.

mira qué clara está la noche ahora,
mira que yo te quiero, que es verdad,
mira cómo donde hubo
parcelas hay llanuras,
mira a tu hijo que vuelve
sin camino y sin manta, como entonces,
a tu regazo con remordimiento.

Come, see how the night is bright now,
see that I love you, that I do indeed.
See how where once there was acreage
now there are open fields,
see how your son comes back
without road or blanket, as then,
with remorse to your knee.

CIELO

AHORA necesito más que nunca
mirar al cielo. Ya sin fe y sin nadie,
tras este seco mediodía, alzo
los ojos. Y es la misma verdad de antes
aunque el testigo sea distinto. Riesgos
de una aventura sin leyendas ni ángeles,
ni siquiera ese azul que hay en mi patria.
Vale dinero respirar el aire,
alzar los ojos, ver sin recompensa,
aceptar una gracia que no cabe
en los sentidos pero les da nueva
salud, los aligera y puebla. Vale
por mi amor este don, esta hermosura
que no merezco ni merece nadie.
Hoy necesito el cielo más que nunca.
No que me salve, sí que me acompañe.

SKY

NOW more than ever I need to look
at the sky. Now without faith or friends,
after this dry midday I look up.
And it's the same truth as before,
although the witness has changed.
Risk of adventure without legends or angels,
or even that blue of my native land.
It's worth money to breathe this air,
raise my eyes and see without return,
accept a blessing that won't fit in the senses,
but that gives them renewed health,
lightens them and makes its home there.
This gift is worth my love, a beauty
neither I nor anyone deserves.
Today I need the sky more than ever,
not to save me but to keep me company.

AJENO

LARGO se le hace el día a quien no ama
y él lo sabe. Y él oye ese tañido
corto y duro del cuerpo, su cascada
canción, siempre sonando a lejanía.
Cierra su puerta y queda bien cerrada;
sale y, por un momento, sus rodillas
se le van hacia el suelo. Pero el alba,
con peligrosa generosidad,
le refresca y le yergue. Está muy clara
su calle y la pasea con pie oscuro,
y cojea en seguida porque anda
sólo con su fatiga. Y dice aire:
palabras muertas con su boca viva.
Prisionero por no querer abraza
su propia soledad. Y está seguro,
más seguro que nadie porque nada
poseerá; y él bien sabe que nunca
vivirá aquí, en la tierra. A quien no ama,
¿cómo podemos conocer o cómo
perdonar? Día largo y aún más larga
la noche. Mentirá al sacar la llave.
Entrará. Y nunca habitará su casa.

A STRANGER

T H E day is long for the one who can't love
and who knows it. And he hears the harsh
tune in his body, its rasping song,
always with the sound of distance.
He closes his door and it stays tight shut;
he goes out, and for a moment his knees
bend and take him to the ground.
But the dawn, with dangerous generosity,
refreshes and sets him on his feet.
His street is bright and he walks it
with somber tread, and he limps along
because fatigue is his only burden.
He says air: dead words from his crafty mouth.
A prisoner because he cannot love,
he embraces his solitude. And he is certain,
more certain than anyone, because
there is nothing he will ever own,
and he knows he can never live in this land.
How can we ever know or pardon
the one who doesn't love? His days are long
and his nights are longer still.
He will lie when he takes out his key.
He will enter and never be at home.

B I E N sé yo cómo luce
la flor por la Sanabria,
cerca de Portugal, en tierras pobres
de producción y de consumo
mas de gran calidad de trigo y trino.
No es el recuerdo tuyo. Hoy es tan sólo
la empresa, la aventura,
no la memoria lo que busco. Es esa
tensión de la distancia,
el fiel kilometraje. No, no quiero
la duración, la garantía de una
imagen, hoy holgada y ya mañana
fruncida. Quiero ver aquel terreno,
pisar la ruta inolvidable, oír
el canto de la luz aquella, ver
cómo el amor, las lluvias
tempranas hoy han hecho
estos lodos, vivir
esa desenvoltura de la brisa
que allí corre. No, hoy no
lucho ya con tu cuerpo
sino con el camino que a él me lleva.
Quiero que mis sentidos,
sin ti, me sigan siendo de provecho.
Entre una parada
y otra saludar a aquellos hombres
para ver lo que soy capaz de dar

94

TOWARD A MEMORY

YES, I know there are flowers
now, near Portugal, in Sanabria:
that region of slight production
and consumption, but with wheat
and warbling of high quality. It's
not your memory. Today it's
the challenge, the expectation,
not the memory, I'm after: the
suspense of the distance, the faithful
miles. Not the permanence
or the promise of your likeness,
faithful today but wrinkled tomorrow.
I want to see that land, walk
those unforgettable paths,
hear the song of that light,
see how love and early rain
have brought us this silt,
live again in that rustling breeze.
I don't struggle now with your body,
but with the paths leading me there.
And even with you gone
I'll still need all my senses.
Between one stop and another
I call to some workmen to see
what I can give and receive,
what to throw away, what can
still be of use. I want to enter a city,

y capaz de aceptar,
para ver qué desecho
qué es lo que aún me es útil,
entrar en las ciudades, respirar
con aliento natal en ellas sean
las que fueren. No busco
masticar esa seca
tajada del recuerdo,
comprar esa quincalla, urdir tan pobre
chapuza. Busco el sitio, la distancia,
el hormigón vibrado y tenso, la única
compañía gentil, la que reúne
tanta vida dispersa. No tan sólo
tu carne que ahora ya arde como estopa
y de la que soy llama,
sino el calibre puro, el área misma
de tu separación y de la tierra.
De aquella tierra donde el sol madura
lo que no dura.

any one at all, and breathe
the air there like a native son.
I don't want to chew the stale
slice of memory, buy tinker's
wares or worthless tin. I only
look for the place, the distance,
the shimmering pavement,
for those worthwhile friends
who'd bring us all together.
It's not your flesh that burns
like hemp for which I'm the flame,
but the miles, the measure
of your distance and the land's,
that land where the sun ripens
what doesn't endure.

ACOSTUMBRADOS a los días, hechos
a su oscuro aposento palmo a palmo,
¿a qué nos viene ahora
este momento? Quién iba a esperarlo
y menos hoy aún lunes y tan lejos
de la flor del jornal. Y, sin embargo,
más que otras veces ahora es tan sencillo
hacer amigos. Basta un gesto llano
y esta región inmensa y sin conquista
que es el hombre, héla: nuestra. Tras tanto
concierto de cuartel he aquí la música
del corazón por un momento. Algo
luce tan de repente que nos ciega
pero sentimos que no luce en vano.
Acostumbrados a los días como
a la respiración, suena tan claro
este momento en nuestra sorda vida
que, ¿qué hay que hacer, si aún están los labios
sucios para besar, si aún están fríos
nuestros brazos?
¿Dónde, dónde hay que ir? ¿Fuera de casa
o aquí, aquí, techo abajo?

A MOMENT

s o familiar with the days,
slowly formed by the contours
of their dark chambers,
why the gift of this moment now?
Who would have expected it
and much less today, Monday,
so far from our next day of rest.
And still, more than ever before,
it's so easy to make friends.
It only takes one welcoming gesture
and this vast, unconquered
region of mankind is suddenly
ours. After so much military
fanfare here for a moment
is music of the heart; and
something blazes so suddenly
that it blinds us but we know
it hasn't blazed in vain.
As familiar with the days
as with breathing, this moment
rings clearly in our deaf lives,
but what can we do with lips
that are too stale for kissing,
with arms that are still cold?
Where, where should we go?
Out of doors or under this roof?

Ahora ya o todo o nada. De mí, de estos
amigos, de esta luz que no da abasto
para tanto vivir, de nuestros días
idos, de nuestro tiempo acribillado,
hay que sacar la huella aunque sea un trazo
tan sólo, un manchón lóbrego
de sombrío pulgar, aunque sea al cabo
por un momento, éste de ahora, y nadie
jamás sea su amo
mientras, luz en la luz, se nos va. Y vuelve,
vuelve lo acostumbrado.

Now it's all or nothing.
We must gather the prints,
if only the smudge, the trace
of a somber thumb: my prints
and those of our friends,
the prints of this light that
isn't enough for so much life,
the prints of our bygone days,
of our pockmarked time;
even if these prints only
last for a moment,
this one now, that none
should command,
while this light in the light
leaves. And the familiar
returns, it returns.

H O Y con el viento del Norte
me ha venido aquella historia.
Mal andaban por entonces
mis pies y peor mi boca
en aquella ciudad de hosco
censo, de miseria y de honra.
Entre la vieja costumbre
de rapiña y de lisonja,
de pobre encuesta y de saldo
barato, iba ya muy coja
mi juventud. ¿Por qué lo hice?
Me avergüenzo de mi boca
no por aquellas palabras
sino por aquella boca
que besó. ¿Qué tiempo hace
de ello? ¿Quién me lo reprocha?
Un sabor a almendra amarga
queda, un sabor a carcoma;
sabor a traición, a cuerpo
vendido, a caricia pocha.

Ojalá el tiempo tan sólo
fuera lo que se ama. Se odia
y es tiempo también. Y es canto.
Te odié entonces y hoy me importa
recordarte, verte enfrente
sin que nadie nos socorra

A MEAN-SPIRITED TIME

TODAY with the north wind
I remembered that affair.
Back when my feet misled me
and my mouth even more,
in that city of flawed census,
misery and honor.
Between timeworn rituals
of thievery and flattery,
of fire sales and easy installments,
my youth already limped along.
Why did I do it? I'm ashamed:
not for the words I spoke
but for the mouth I kissed.
How long ago was it now?
How was I to blame? It left
a taste of bitter almond,
of termite-eaten wood,
a taste of betrayal, of a body
sold, a rotten caress.

I wish it were only time
that we love. But we hate
and that's also time. And song.
I hated you then and today
I need to remember you,
see you before me with

y amarte otra vez y odiarte
de nuevo. Te beso ahora
y te traiciono ahora sobre
tu cuerpo. ¿Quién no negocia
con lo poco que posee?
Si ayer fue venta hoy es compra;
mañana, arrepentimiento.
No es la sola hora la aurora.

no one to save us; to love you
again and to hate you again.
I'd kiss you now but betray
your body. Who doesn't
bargain with the little they have?
If yesterday we sold, today we buy,
tomorrow we repent.
Dawn is not the only hour.

CUALQUIER cosa valiera por mi vida
esta tarde. Cualquier cosa pequeña
si alguna hay. Martirio me es el ruido
sereno, sin escrúpulos, sin vuelta,
de tu zapato bajo. ¿Qué victorias
busca el que ama? ¿Por qué son tan derechas
estas calles? Ni miro atrás ni puedo
perderte ya de vista. Ésta es la tierra
del escarmiento: hasta los amigos
dan mala información. Mi boca besa
lo que muere, y lo acepta. Y la piel misma
del labio es la del viento. Adiós. Es útil,
normal este suceso, dicen. Queda
tú con las cosas nuestras, tú, que puedes,
que yo me iré donde la noche quiera.

GOODBYE

I'D take anything for my life
this afternoon. Any small token
if there is one. It's martyrdom,
the calm, determined,
unforgiving sound of your steps.
What victory do lovers seek?
Why are these streets so straight?
I don't look back but I'll always see you.
This is a punishing land: even friends
misinform. My mouth kisses what's dying
and accepts it. The very skin of my lips
is the wind's. Goodbye. What's happened
is useful they say, a normal event.
You, remain with our things, you who can,
while I go wherever the night takes me.

BIENVENIDA la noche para quien va seguro
y con los ojos claros mira sereno el campo,
y con la vida limpia mira con paz el cielo,
su ciudad y su casa, su familia y su obra.

Pero a quien anda a tientas y ve sombra, ve el duro
ceño del cielo y vive la condena de su tierra
y la malevolencia de sus seres queridos,
enemiga es la noche y su piedad acoso.

Y aún más en este páramo de la alta Rioja
donde se abre con tanta claridad que deslumbra,
palpita tan cercana que sobrecoge y muy
en el alma se entra, y la remueve a fondo.

Porque la noche siempre, como el fuego, revela,
refina, pule el tiempo, la oración y el sollozo,
da tersura al pecado, limpidez al recuerdo,
castigando y salvando toda una vida entera.

Bienvenida la noche con su peligro hermoso.

W E L C O M E is the night for the one who goes in safety,
and with clear eyes looks serenely on the fields,
and with a clean life looks peacefully at the sky,
at his city, his house, his family and his labor.

But for one who gropes his way and sees shadows, sees
the sky's dark frown, bears the curse of his homeland,
and the maliciousness of his loved ones,
the night is an enemy and its pity a siege.

Especially here in the north Rioja highlands,
where night comes on with a brightness that dazzles,
and throbs from so close that it frightens and enters
deeply into the soul and stirs it profoundly.

Because the night, like fire, always illumines,
refines, polishes time and prayers and sobbing,
gives sin a hard surface and clarity to memories,
punishing and salvaging the whole of our life.

Welcome is the night with its lovely danger.

E L dolor verdadero no hace ruido.
Deja un susurro como el de las hojas
del álamo mecidas por el viento,
un rumor entrañable, de tan honda
vibración, tan sensible al menor roce,
que puede hacerse soledad, discordia,
injusticia o despecho. Estoy oyendo
su murmurado son que no alborota
sino que da armonía, tan buido
y sutil, tan timbrado de espaciosa
serenidad, en medio de esta tarde,
que casi es ya cordura dolorosa,
pura resignación. Traición que vino
de un ruin consejo de la seca boca
de la envidia. Es lo mismo. Estoy oyendo
lo que me obliga y me enriquece a costa
de heridas que aún supuran. Dolor que oigo
muy recogidamente como a fronda
mecida sin buscar señas, palabras
o significación. Música sola,
sin enigmas, son solo que traspasa
mi corazón, dolor que es mi victoria.

LIKE THE SOUND OF POPLAR LEAVES

TRUE sorrow doesn't make noise.
Only a soft whisper like the sound
of poplar leaves swayed by the wind,
a sound so intimate, so tremulous,
so sensitive to the slightest touch
that it may become solitude, discord,
injustice, resentment. I hear its
murmured tune that doesn't dismay,
but is a harmony so subtle and slender
in tone, so stamped with spacious
serenity on this mid-afternoon,
that it's almost painful wisdom,
pure resignation, betrayal,
malicious advice from the dry mouth
of envy. It's all the same. I listen
to what compels and enriches me
at the cost of still festering wounds.
Sorrow I listen to with reverence
as though to stirring leaves,
without searching for signs
or words or meaning. Only for music,
without mystery, only for sound
that pierces my heart, sorrow that's my victory.

¿QUÉ clara contraseña
me ha abierto lo escondido? ¿Qué aire viene
y con delicadeza cautelosa
deja en el cuerpo su honda carga y toca
con tino vehemente ese secreto
quicio de los sentidos donde tiembla
la nueva acción, la nueva
alianza? Da dicha
y ciencia este suceso. Y da aventura
en medio de hospitales,
de bancos y autobuses a la diaria
rutina. Ya han pasado
los años y aún no puede
pagar todas sus deudas
mi juventud. Pero ahora
este tesoro, este
olor, que es mi verdad,
que es mi alegría y mi arrepentimiento,
me madura y me alza.

Olor a sal, a cuero y a canela,
a lana burda y a pizarra, acaso
algo ácido, transido
de familiaridad y de sorpresa.
¿Qué materia ha cuajado
en la ligera ráfaga que ahora
trae lo perdido y trae

A SMELL

WHAT clear countersign
has opened what was hidden? What
breeze comes and with cautious delicacy
leaves a profound gift in my body,
touching with vehement exactness
that secret hinge of the senses, where
the new act trembles, the new alliance?
This event brings happiness and wisdom,
and adds adventure among hospitals,
banks and buses to the daily routine.
Many years have gone by
and my youth hasn't paid all its debts.
But now this treasure, this smell
that's my truth, my happiness
and repentance, matures and lifts me.

A smell of salt, leather and cinnamon,
rough wool and slate: perhaps a little bitter,
touched with intimacy and surprise. What
substance has become this faint gust
that brings me what was lost
and what was won,
brings time and memories,

lo ganado, trae tiempo
y trae recuerdo y trae
libertad y condena?
Gracias doy a este soplo
que huele a un cuerpo amado y a una tarde
y a una ciudad, a este aire
íntimo de erosión que cala a fondo
y me trabaja silenciosamente
dándome aroma y tufo.
A este olor que es mi vida.

freedom and condemnation?
I give thanks to this gentle
breeze that smells of a beloved body,
of an afternoon and a city,
to this intimate air of erosion
that enters so deeply and works
in me quietly, that brings me
this fragrance and this odor,
this smell that's my life.

SIN LEYES

Ya cantan los gallos,
amor mío. Vete:
cata que amanece.

ANÓNIMO

EN esta cama donde el sueño es llanto,
no de reposo, sino de jornada,
nos ha llegado la alta noche. ¿El cuerpo
es la pregunta o la respuesta a tanta
dicha insegura? Tos pequeña y seca,
pulso que viene fresco ya y apaga
la vieja ceremonia de la carne
mientras no quedan gestos ni palabras
para volver a interpretar la escena
como noveles. Te amo. Es la hora mala
de la cruel cortesía. Tan presente
te tengo siempre que mi cuerpo acaba
en tu cuerpo moreno por el que una
vez más me pierdo, por el que mañana
me perderé. Como una guerra sin
héroes, como una paz sin alianzas,
ha pasado la noche. Y yo te amo.
Busco despojos, busco una medalla
rota, un trofeo vivo de este tiempo
que nos quieren robar. Estás cansada
y yo te amo. Es la hora. ¿Nuestra carne
será la recompensa, la metralla

BEYOND RULES

The cocks already crow,
my love. Go now.
Be careful, it's morning.
ANONYMOUS

I N this bed where sleep is sobbing,
not from our rest but our long march,
we've reached the middle of the night.
Is the body a question or an answer
for so much cautious happiness?
A small dry cough, a fresh new pulse
that ends the old ceremony of the flesh,
now that we've no more words or gestures
to play our parts again like novices.
I love you. Now's the sad hour
of cruel courtesy.
But I'm so aware of you
my body always ends
in your dark body,
where now I lose my way,
where tomorrow I'll lose my way again.
Like a battle without heroes,
a peace without alliances,
we've passed the night. And I love you.
I look for spoils, for a broken
medal, for any living trophy
of this time they mean to steal.

que justifique tanta lucha pura
sin vencedores ni vencidos? Calla,
que yo te amo. Es la hora. Entra ya un trémulo
albor. Nunca la luz fue tan temprana.

You're tired and I love you. It's time.
Will our bodies be the reparations
or debris that justify this perfect
warfare without victory or defeat?
Hush. I truly love you. It's time.
Daylight begins to filter through.
Never has morning come this soon.

DENTRO de poco saldrá el sol. El viento,
aún con su fresca suavidad nocturna,
lava y aclara el sueño y da viveza,
incertidumbre a los sentidos. Nubes
de pardo ceniciento, azul turquesa,
por un momento traen quietud, levantan
la vida y engrandecen su pequeña
luz. Luz que pide, tenue y tierna, pero
venturosa, porque ama. Casi a medio
camino entre la noche y la mañana,
cuando todo me acoge, cuando hasta
mi corazón me es muy amigo, ¿cómo
puedo dudar, no bendecir el alba
si aún en mi cuerpo hay juventud y hay
en mis labios amor?

DAYBREAK

S O O N the sun will rise. The wind,
still with its fresh nocturnal softness,
washes and rinses my sleep, quickens
and confounds the senses. Ashen brown
clouds, turquoise blue clouds,
bring a momentary stillness, quicken
life and increase its faint light. This light
that begs, tentative and tender, yet
fortunate too because it loves. Nearly
halfway between night and morning,
when everything welcomes me
and even my heart is a good friend,
how can I doubt, not bless this dawn,
if there is still youth in my body
and love on my lips?

DÉJAME que te hable en esta hora
de dolor con alegres
palabras. Ya se sabe
que el escorpión, la sanguijuela, el piojo,
curan a veces. Pero tú oye, déjame
decirte que, a pesar
de tanta vida deplorable, sí,
a pesar y aun ahora
que estamos en derrota, nunca en doma,
el dolor es la nube,
la alegría, el espacio,
el dolor es el huésped,
la alegría, la casa.
Que el dolor es la miel,
símbolo de la muerte, y la alegría
es agria, seca, nueva,
lo único que tiene
verdadero sentido.
Déjame que con vieja
sabiduría, diga:
a pesar, a pesar
de todos los pesares
y aunque sea muy dolorosa y aunque
sea a veces inmunda, siempre, siempre
la más honda verdad es la alegría.
La que de un río turbio
hace aguas limpias,

NOT A DREAM

L E T me, in this hour of sorrow,
say joyful words to you.
We know that scorpions, leeches,
lice sometimes cure. But listen,
let me tell you that despite
so much reprehensible life
—and yes, despite it and even
now when we're overrun
but not subdued—
that sorrow is a cloud
but joy is space,
that sorrow is the guest
and joy the house,
that sorrow is honey,
a symbol of death,
and joy is bitter, dry, new,
the only thing
that truly makes sense.
With ancient wisdom let me say
that despite, despite it all,
and although
it's so very sorrowful,
even at times obscene,
that always, always,
the deepest truth is joy.
It makes clear water
of a muddy river,

la que hace que te diga
estas palabras tan indignas ahora,
la que nos llega como
llega la noche y llega la mañana,
como llega a la orilla
la ola:
irremediablemente.

it makes me say these unworthy words,
it's what comes as night comes
and as morning comes,
as waves come to the shore:
irremediably.

UNA LUZ

E S T A luz cobre, la que más me ayuda
en tareas de amor y de sosiego,
me saca fuerzas de flaqueza. Este
beneficio que de vicioso aliento
hace rezo, cariño de lascivia,
y alza de la ceniza llama, y da
a la sal alianza; estos minutos
que protegen, montan y ensamblan treinta
años, poniendo en ellos sombra y mimo,
perseverancia y humildad y agudo
sacrificio, esta gracia, esta hermosura,
esta tortura que me da en la cara,
luz tan mía, tan fiel siempre y tan poco
duradera, por la que sé que soy
sencillo de reseña, por la que ahora
vivo sin andamiajes, sin programas,
sin repertorios. A esta luz yo quiero,
de tan cárdena, cobre. Luz que toma
cuerpo en mí, tiempo en mí, luz que es mi vida
porque me da la vida: lo que pido
para mi amor y para mi sosiego.

THIS LIGHT

T H I S copper light, that helps me most
in love's labors and at ease,
lifts me when I'm low. This bounty
that turns my flawed breath into prayer,
my lust to affection, raises flames
from ashes, offers salt an alliance;
these minutes that shelter, assemble,
fasten thirty years, filling them with shadow,
tenderness, humility, perseverance,
painful sacrifice; this grace, this loveliness,
this torture that falls across my face,
this light so mine, so ever-faithful
yet so short-lived,
that tells me I'm an easy study,
that now I live without programs,
scaffoldings or repertoire. I love this light
for its purple, copper hue.
Light that takes shape in me,
that is time in me,
this light that is my life
because it gives me life:
all I ask for my love and my case.

A veces, mal vestido un bien nos viene;
casi sin ropa, sin acento, como
de una raza bastarda. Y cuando llega
tras tantas horas deslucidas, pronto
a dar su gracia, no sabemos nunca
qué hacer ni cómo saludar ni cómo
distinguir su hacendoso laboreo
de nuestra poca maña. ¿Estamos sordos
a su canción tan susurrada, pobre
de notas? Quiero ver, pedirte ese oro
que cae de tus bolsillos y me paga
todo el vivir, bien que entras silencioso
en la esperanza, en el recuerdo, por
la puerta de servicio, y eres sólo
el temblor de una hoja, el dar la mano
con fe, la levadura de estos ojos
a los que tú haces ver las cosas claras,
lejanas de su muerte, sin el moho
de su destino y su misterio. Pisa
mi casa al fin, recórrela, que todo
te esperaba. Yo quiero que tu huella
pasajera, tu visitarme hermoso,
no se me vayan más, como otras veces
que te volví la cara en un otoño
cárdeno, como el de hoy, y te dejaba
morir en tus pañales luminosos.

A GIFT

SOMETIMES in tatters a gift arrives,
all unassuming, of an unknown race.
And when it appears, all eager to please,
after spiritless days, we never know
what to do, how to greet it, how to tell
its eager service from our awkwardness.
Are we deaf to its whispered tune
of so few notes? I want to see, ask for
the gold that spills from your pockets,
and pays for all my years, even though
you enter my hopes, my memories
quietly by the servants' door, and
are no more than a trembling leaf,
a forthright handshake, leaven for my
eyes to help me see things clearly,
far from their death and without the mold
of their destiny and their mystery. Enter
my house at last, go upstairs and down,
everything is waiting. I don't want
your hasty steps, your lovely visiting,
ever to leave me again, as so often before
when I turned my back, one crimson
autumn like today, and left you to die
in your radiant swaddling clothes.

IV

ODA A LA NIÑEZ

I

¿Y ésta es tu bienvenida,
marzo, para salir de casa alegres:
con viento húmedo y frío de meseta?
Siempre ahora, en la puerta,
y aún a pesar nuestro, vuelve, vuelve
este destino de niñez que estalla
por todas partes: en la calle, en esta
voraz respiración del día, en la
sencillez del primer humo sabroso,
en la mirada, en cada laboreo
del hombre.
Siempre así, de vencida,
sólo por miedo a tal castigo, a tal
combate, ahora hacemos
confuso vocerío por ciudades,
por fábricas, por barrios
de vecindad. Mas tras la ropa un tiemblo
nos tañe y al salir por tantas calles
sin piedad y sin bulla
rompen claras escenas
de amanecida y tantos
sucios ladrillos sin salud se cuecen
de intimidad de lecho y guiso. Entonces,
nada hay que nos aleje
de nuestro hondo oficio de inocencia;

ODE TO CHILDHOOD

I

A N D is this your welcome, March,
as we step happily out of doors
into the damp chill wind of the highlands?
Always now on our doorstep,
suddenly, and even despite ourselves,
our vocation for childhood erupts
all around us. It returns, it returns:
in streets, in the insatiable breath of day,
in the purity of the first sweet-tasting smoke,
in our gaze, in every undertaking
of mankind.
Always this way, at a loss,
for fear of this punishment,
this combat, our voices
clamor in cities, in factories,
in neighborhoods. But through our clothing
we sense a tremor, and as we walk
so many still, pitiless streets,
bright morning scenes
unfold around us
and so many crumbling,
ailing bricks begin to cook
with the snug intimacy
of beds and meals.
Then nothing can keep us

entonces, ya en faena,
cruzamos esta plaza con pie nuevo
y, aun entre la ventisca, como si en junio fuera,
se abre nuestro pulmón trémulo de alba
y, como a mediodía,
ricos son nuestros ojos
de oscuro señorío.

II

Muchos hombres pasaron junto a nosotros, pero
no eran de nuestro pueblo.
Arrinconadas vidas dejan por estos barrios,
ellos, que eran el barrio sin murallas.
Miraron, y no vieron; ni verdad ni mentira
sino vacía bagatela
desearon, vivieron. Culpa ha sido
de todos el que oyesen
tan sólo el ciego pulso
de la injusticia, la sangrienta marcha
del casco frío del rencor. La puesta
del sol fue sólo puesta
del corazón. ¿Qué hacen ahí las palmas
de esos balcones sin el blanco lazo
de nuestra honda orfandad? ¿Qué este mercado
por donde paso ahora,
los cuarteles, las fábricas, las nubes,
la vida, el aire, todo,

from our profound vocation of innocence
as, eager for work to begin,
we take fresh steps across the square,
and even in a blizzard, as though it were June,
our trembling lungs begin to swell with morning,
and just as at noon our eyes
are rich with a mysterious
dominion.

11

Many people passed through
but were never of this village.
They left us with their shoved-aside lives,
although they were a neighborhood without walls.
They looked and didn't see, didn't hope
for truth or lies, only hoped for, lived for,
meaningless trifles. We were all to blame
that they only heard the blind pulse
of injustice, the bloody clip-clop
of the cold hooves of hatred.
A setting sun was only
a sundown of the heart.
Why are there palms on balconies
without the white ribbons
of our profound orphanhood?
And what of this market
I walk through today,
these barracks, factories, clouds,

sin la borrasca de nuestra niñez
que alza ola para siempre?
Siempre al salir pensamos
en la distancia, nunca
en la compañía. Y cualquier sitio es bueno
para hacer amistades.
Aunque hoy es peligroso. Mucho polvo
entre los pliegues de la propaganda
hay. Cuanto antes
lleguemos al trabajo, mejor. Mala
bienvenida la tuya, marzo. Y nuestras calles,
claras como si dieran a los campos,
¿adónde dan ahora? ¿Por qué todo es infancia?
Mas ya la luz se amasa,
poco a poco enrojece, el viento templa
y en sus cosechas vibra
un grano de alianza, un cabeceo
de los inmensos pastos del futuro.

III

Una verdad se ha dicho sin herida,
sin el negocio sucio
de las lágrimas,
con la misma ternura con que se da la nieve.

this life, this air, this all,
without the tempest of our childhood
to drive the waves along forever?
When we start out
we always think of the distance,
never of our companions,
and anywhere is fine for making friends,
although that's dangerous today.
There is so much dust in the pages of propaganda
that the sooner we reach our workplace, the better.
Yours is an unkind welcome, March.
And our streets are as bright
as though they opened on outlying fields.
On what do they open now?
Why is everything childhood?
But daylight already thickens,
little by little turns red,
the wind dies
and in its harvests
a seed of alliance trembles,
with the swaying wheat
of the vast pastures of the future.

III

A truth was spoken without wounding,
without the dirty business of tears,
with the same tenderness as falling snow.
See how everything is childhood:

Ved que todo es infancia.
La fidelidad de la tierra,
la presencia del cielo insoportable
que se nos cuela aquí, hasta en la cazalla
mañanera, los días
que amanecen con trinos y anochecen
con gárgaras, el ruido
del autobús que por fin llega, nuestras
palabras que ahora,
al saludar, quisieran
ser panales y son
telas de araña, nuestra
violencia hereditaria,
la droga del recuerdo, la alta estafa del tiempo,
la dignidad del hombre
que hay que abrazar y hay
que ofrecer y hay
que salvar aquí mismo,
en medio de esta lluvia fría de marzo...
Ved que todo es infancia:
la verdad que es silencio para siempre.
Años de compra y venta,
hombres llenos de precios,
los pregones sin voz, las turbias bodas,
nos trajeron el miedo a la gran aventura
de nuestra raza, a la niñez. Ah, quietos,

the faithfulness of the earth,
the unbearable presence of the sky
that even elbows its way
into our morning *cazalla*,
the days that begin with birdsong
and end with gargling,
the noise of the bus
that finally arrives, the words of greeting
that wish they were honeycombs
but are cobwebs,
our hereditary violence,
the drug of memory, the ruinous swindle of time,
the dignity of mankind that we must embrace
and offer and salvage,
here in this cold March rain...
See how everything is childhood,
a truth that was always silenced.
Years of buying and selling,
men covered with prices,
voiceless huckstering, hasty weddings,
made us afraid of childhood,
the great adventure of our race.
Steady, hold still for the iron
that brands and heals and masters us.
A master that's grateful service,
bridles that will make us brothers.

quietos bajo ese hierro
que nos marca, y nos sana, y nos da amo.
Amo que es servidumbre, bridas que nos hermanan.

IV

Y nos lo quitarán todo
menos estas
botas de siete leguas.
Aquí, aquí, bien calzadas
en nuestros sosos pies de paso corto.
Aquí, aquí, estos zapatos
diarios, los de la ventana
del seis de enero.
Y nos lo quitarán todo
menos el traje sucio
de comunión, éste, el de siempre, el puesto.
Lo de entonces fue sueño. Fue una edad. Lo de ahora
no es presente o pasado,
ni siquiera futuro: es el origen.
Ésta es la única hacienda
del hombre. Y cuando estamos
llegando y ya la lluvia
zozobra en nubes rápidas y se hunde
por estos arrabales
trémula de estertores luminosos,
bajamos la cabeza
y damos gracias sin saber qué es ello,

IV

And they'll take all away
but our seven-league boots.
Yes, yes, a good fit
for our slow-moving feet.
Yes, these everyday shoes
that we set in our window
for January Sixth.
And they'll take all away
but our stained communion suit,
this one that we wear every day.
The other was a dream, of another age.
This one isn't present or past
or even the future: it's the source.
This is man's only treasure.
And when we're almost there
and rain filters through
the streaming clouds,
drowning the vacant lots
and trembling
with shimmering eager breath,
we bow our heads and give thanks
without knowing what this is,

qué es lo que pasa, quién a sus maneras
nos hace, qué herrería,
qué inmortal fundición es ésta. Y nadie,
nada hay que nos aleje
de nuestro oficio de felicidad
sin distancia ni tiempo.
Es el momento ahora
en el que, quién lo diría, alto, ciego, renace
el sol primaveral de la inocencia,
ya sin ocaso sobre nuestra tierra.

what's happening,
who bends us to their will,
what forge, what immortal foundry
this is. And there's no one,
nothing that can keep us
from our craft of happiness
without distance or time.
This is the moment now
—who would believe it?—
when the high, blind, dazzling,
spring-like sun
of innocence is reborn,
never to set again on our land.

I

EN cualquier tiempo y en cualquier terreno
siempre hay un hombre que
anda tan vagabundo como el humo,
bienhechor, malhechor,
bautizado con la agria
leche de nuestras leyes. Y él encuentra
su salvación en
la hospitalidad.
Como la ropa atrae a la polilla,
como el amor a toda
su parentela de lujuria y gracia,
de temor y de dicha,
así una casa le seduce. Y no
por ser panal o ancla
sino por ese oscuro
divorcio entre el secuestro de sus años,
la honda cautividad del tiempo ido
ahí, entre las paredes,
y su maltrecha libertad de ahora.
Forastero, ve cómo
una vieja mentira se hace una verdad nueva.
Ve el cuerpo del engaño
y lo usa: esa puerta
que, al abrirse, rechina
con cruel desconfianza, con amargo reproche;

ODE TO HOSPITALITY

I

I N any time and on any ground
there is always a man who wanders,
as vagabond as smoke,
who authors good deeds, bad deeds,
who was baptized in the sour
milk of our laws. And he finds
salvation
in hospitality.
Just as wool attracts moths,
and love its kin of sensuality
and grace, fear and delight,
one house will beguile him.
Not because it's honeycomb or anchor,
but for the dark divorce
between his sequestered years,
the grim captivity of the time
he spent between those walls,
and his present knockabout freedom.
A stranger, he sees how an old lie
becomes a new truth;
despite the house's deceit
he enters by a door that creaks
with cruel suspicion, with bitter reproach;
he sees a window —where dry almond blossoms
still recall spring— that seems a blank wall,

esa ventana donde
la flor quemada del almendro aún deja
primavera, y le es muro,
y su cristal esclavitud, las tejas
ya sin musgo ni fe,
el mobiliario de diseño tan
poco amigo, la loza
fría y rebelde cuando
antes le fue recreo y muchas veces
hasta consuelo, el cuarto familiar
de humildad agresiva, recogiendo,
malogrando
lo que una boca muy voluble y muy
dolorosa, hace años
pronunció, silenció, besó… Ésta es la lucha, éste
es el tiempo, el terreno
donde él ha de vencer si es que no busca
recuerdos y esperanzas
tan sólo. Si es que busca
fundación, servidumbre.

II

Y hoy, como la lluvia
lava la hoja, esta mañana clara,
tan abrileña prematuramente,
limpia de polvo y de oropeles tanto
tiempo, y germina y crea
casi un milagro de hechos y sucesos,

and its glass, his slavery;
he sees roof tiles
with no moss or faith,
the matching, unfriendly furniture,
the china, cold and rebellious
when often before it pleased,
even comforted him;
the parlor, aggressively
humble, gathering, distorting
what a garrulous, saddened
mouth spoke, silenced, kissed,
many years ago... Here is the battle,
the moment, the ground
where he has to make a stand,
if he's not looking only
for memories and hope,
but for foundation, grateful servitude.

II

And just as rain washes leaves,
today this cloudless morning
—so very like early April—
cleans tinsel and dust
from so much time,
creates and makes sprout

y remacha y ajusta
tanta vida ambulante, tanta fortuna y fraude
a través de los días
purificando rostros y ciudades,
dando riqueza a una menesterosa
juventud, preparando,
situando el vivir. ¿Mas alguien puede
hacer de su pasado
simple materia de revestimiento:
cera, laca, barniz, lo que muy pronto
se marchita, tan pronto
como la flor del labio?
¿O bien ha de esperar a estar con esos
verdaderos amigos, los que darán sentido
a su vida, a su tierra y a su casa?

III

Es la hospitalidad. Es el origen
de la fiesta y del canto.
Porque el canto es tan sólo
palabra hospitalaria: la que salva
aunque deje la herida. Y el amor es tan sólo
herida hospitalaria, aunque no tenga cura,
y la libertad cabe
en una humilde mano hospitalaria,

a near miracle of deeds and events,
adjusts and clinches
so much errant life,
so much fortune and fraud
for so many days,
refining faces and cities,
providing an indigent youth
with riches, preparing
and centering life.
But can anyone
limit their past
to a plain surface finish
of wax, lacquer, varnish,
to what will soon fade,
as quickly as the lips' petals?
Or should he wait to be
with those genuine friends who'll give meaning
to his life, his homeland and his house?

III

It's hospitality, it's the source
of feasting and song.
Because song is only hospitable
words that heal
although the wound remains.
And love is a truly hospitable wound
although there's no cure;
and liberty fits

quizá dolida y trémula
mas fundadora y fiel, tendida en servidumbre
y en confianza, no en
sumisión o dominio.
A pesar de que hagamos
de convivencia técnicas
de opresión y medidas
de seguridad y
de la hospitalidad hospicios, siempre
hay un hombre sencillo y una mañana clara,
con la alta transparencia de esta tierra,
y una casa, y una hora
próspera. Y este hombre
ve en torno de la mesa
a sus seres queridos. No pregunta
sino invita, no enseña
vasos de pesadumbre ni vajilla de plata.
Apenas habla y menos
de su destierro.
Lo que esperó lo encuentra
y lo celebra, lejos
el incienso y la pólvora,
aquel dinero, aquel resentimiento.
Ahora su patria es esta generosa
ocasión y, sereno,
algo medroso ante tal bien, acoge
y nombra, uno por uno,
a sus amigos sin linaje, de
nacimiento. Ya nunca
forastero, en familia,

in a humble, hospitable hand
that may ache and tremble
but is foundational, faithful,
offered in grateful service
and with confidence,
not submission or dominion.
Although we make techniques
of oppression and security measures
from conviviality,
hospices from hospitality,
there is always a plain
unassuming man
and a bright morning,
with the supreme transparence of this land,
a house and an auspicious hour.
And this man sees his loved ones
seated at table. He doesn't ask,
he invites. He doesn't set places
with frowning glassware or silver service.
He hardly speaks,
least of all of his exile.
What he hoped for he finds
and celebrates, far from the incense,
the gunpowder, that money
and resentment.
Now his homeland
is this generous occasion,
as calmly, a little frightened
of so much good fortune,
one by one he welcomes

no con docilidad, con aventura,
da las gracias muy a solas,
como mendigo. Y sabe,
comprende al fin. Y mira alegremente,
con esa intimidad de la llaneza
que es la única eficacia,
los rostros y las cosas,
la verdad de su vida
recién ganada aquí, entre las paredes
de una juventud libre y un hogar sin fronteras.

and names his lifelong friends.
Never more a stranger,
among family,
not submissive, with wonder,
he gives solitary thanks
like a beggar. And he knows,
he finally understands, and he looks
with joy, with the intimacy of fellowship
—the only genuine skill—
at the faces and objects,
the truth of his life,
recovered at last between the four walls
of an unbound youth and a limitless hearth.

SWAN ISLE PRESS is an independent, not-for-profit,
literary publisher dedicated to publishing works of poetry,
fiction and nonfiction that inspire and educate while
advancing the knowledge and appreciation of literature,
art, and culture. The Press's bilingual editions and single-
language English translations make contemporary and
classic texts more accessible to a variety of readers.

For more information on books of related interest
or for a catalog of new publications contact:

www.swanislepress.com

ALLIANCE AND CONDEMNATION

—

ALIANZA Y CONDENA

Designed by Andrea Guinn
Typeset in Caslon
Printed on 55# Glatfelter Natural

SWAN
ISLE
PRESS